LIFT YOUR VOICE

DEDICATION

To the memory of my great-grandparents, Hillary Thomas Stewart and Larcenia Stewart, my great-great grandparents, Abraham and Hannah Stewart and Miley and Troy Stewart, who were all born slaves. Even though I never met them, I have realized that my existence today was because of their unyielding faith. I can't even imagine the unthinkable they went through to survive each day as a slave and not as a free person.

I know more than ever the emotional and physical abuse my great-grandparents endured was for their family's future generations to have a better life than they did. When I sometimes look up at the clear blue sky, I visualize their arms wrapped around Perry, saying, "Our world in a better place, my grandson. Our blood, sweat, and tears are worth seeing this change from Heaven."

I cannot forget my parents, Laura Jones Stewart and & H. B. Jones, Sr., who passed many years ago. They taught me how to be proud of what I had, even though it was not much. And of course, my dear sister, Larcenia "Cissy" Jones Floyd, Perry's mother, whose spirit showed up as he yelled out, "Mama, mama" and welcomed him home.

One day, we will all be together.

LIFT YOUR VOICE

HOW MY NEPHEW GEORGE FLOYD'S MURDER CHANGED THE WORLD

ANGELA HARRELSON WITH **MICHAEL LEVIN**

Post Hill
PRESS

A POST HILL PRESS BOOK

Lift Your Voice:
How My Nephew George Floyd's Murder Changed the World
© 2022 by Angela Harrelson with Michael Levin
All Rights Reserved

ISBN: 978-1-63758-337-1
ISBN (eBook): 978-1-63758-338-8

Cover design by Cody Corcoran
Interior design and composition by Greg Johnson, Textbook Perfect

This is a work of nonfiction. All people, locations, events, and situations are portrayed to the best of the author's memory.

Post Hill Press
New York • Nashville
posthillpress.com

Published in the United States of America
1 2 3 4 5 6 7 8 9 10

Contents

CHAPTER 1

"The Police Killed Your Nephew. Do You Have Any Comment?"

The world knows him as George Floyd, but in our family, we all called him Perry. That's because his father was known as George Perry Floyd Senior, and he was known as Perry. So when his son came along, everybody called him Perry too.

I'm twelve years older than Perry, and I first met him when I was sixteen and he was around four. Sometimes his mother (my older sister Larcenia Jones Floyd, whom we called Cissy) would fall on hard times financially, and she and her kids would come to stay with us. This happened several times. Perry was the sweetest boy. Super high energy. Always running around, and never with a shirt on! It was the South, it was hot, and he just liked to charge around. It was great for Perry, his siblings, and his mother to stay with us because they lived in an apartment, where you're always cooped up, so Perry could enjoy himself with us out in the country.

I'm telling you, he was just the sweetest little boy. We lived in an old raggedy shack out in the country with no running water, very little electricity, and an outhouse. It was surprising and humbling to see how easily Perry adapted to the more primitive conditions. He never minded using the outhouse or having to pump water for washing.

His father was an amazing musician. Sometimes, he would come over and play music with my mother, Laura Stewart Jones, who was a very fine pianist. She had a piano growing up, and she would put on a music show at the church most years. There was always music in our family, and when Perry Senior and my mother got together to play, it was magical! Not just great—magical. Perry Senior was a musical genius and could have done anything as a musician, but unfortunately, he went down the same path that his son would go down years later. He struggled with his sobriety, and at some point, he disappeared. I heard he was homeless for a long time, but his family found him and helped him get off drugs. He must have gone into rehab because he was clean and led a Christian life for the last years of his life. He gave himself to God and really got his life straight. Perry said he didn't have a close relationship with his father, but for two people who were far apart, they were closer in spirit and life than they both knew. If only they could have found each other.

We were poor, but we had so much love that if any members of our extended family needed help, they could always come to our raggedy shack to live. When I was younger, I couldn't for the life of me understand why so many family members came home to get help, because their homes were better. But as I got older, I knew that they came to our house for love. There were thirteen of us children in the family; a fourteenth, Frank, died as a baby. Most sharecroppers had big families because children meant free labor. Many white farmers loved to see us coming because they knew we would get a lot of work done!

But at the same time, we had a lot of fun. We had an old black-and-white television, and sometimes we would look at *The Flip*

Wilson Show. That was my favorite '70s show. Perry loved it when Flip was Geraldine, his character about the woman in the bar. Perry didn't know what Flip was saying, but he always laughed and laughed. He actually looked like Flip Wilson! I wanted to put a wig on him so he'd do Geraldine's famous line: "What you see is what you get!"

After I left the house, I moved to Iowa for college. My sister eventually relocated to Texas, and I lost touch with Perry for a number of years. I knew that he was an athlete and a star high school football player, and people thought he had a chance at playing in the NFL. He was six foot four, so he certainly had the size for it! He was also a talented rapper; he performed in shows, and one of his songs became popular in Houston when he lived there. Perry was also a mamma's boy in the best sense of the word: a man who just loved his mom, loved spending time with her, would do anything for her.

By the time I was in my late thirties, we started having big family Thanksgiving dinners every year in Houston. This was really cool because I got a chance to see Perry again. We were always happy to see each other, and I was just happy that his life was turning out okay. My sister, Perry's mom, told me everybody in the community looked up to him because he was such a fine athlete. So it seemed like everything in his life was going right. Then one time, my sister got the courage to tell me the truth: "Perry's in trouble, and he's been in trouble for quite some time. He's not in college anymore. The word on the street is that he's using and doing petty drug deals. He's on the wrong track again."

I remember thinking, "Oh, no, I hope he can get out of this stuff." He really wanted to go to college and finish. It was his dream, and it was also his mother's vision for him. He was trying to do good in the world. He had all the right ingredients, but his mom wasn't healthy and she was going downhill—and she was struggling financially. I guess he thought the petty drugs were the fastest way to make some money to support his family and his drug habit. He probably thought, "If I can help my mom get on her feet, it would help me too. I could get my life out of trouble." As a nurse working with chemical dependency, I can tell you that was a delusion on Perry's part. No one gets out of trouble with drugs like that, even with the best of intentions, which Perry had. The pressures of being in college and trying to help his mom were too much for him.

Perry would always tell me, "I'm going to be all right." He would not go into detail about what he was doing. I think he was ashamed because he'd had so much stature in the community as an athlete and as a pro football prospect and then he lost it all. He fell into an emotional trap.

After Perry left college and returned to Houston, the police wouldn't leave him alone. He served ten months in jail for selling less than a gram of cocaine, and once he had a record, the police harassed him all the time. He was jailed on minor charges such as trespassing repeatedly and served several months for theft, pleading out although the evidence was questionable. Another conviction for selling ten dollars' worth of crack is still under investigation because the arresting officer was suspected of supplying false evidence. Finally, in 2007, Perry was convicted of aggravated robbery and sent to state prison. He was trying to help his family in doing the wrong things for the right reasons. Cissy was devastated.

The police said it was a home invasion, that Perry was in a gang trying to take some drugs from other drug dealers. More than one man hurt the woman in the house, but Perry—the "big guy"—was the only one arrested. He pled out even though the identification was shaky, based on procedures that the Houston Police don't use anymore. Perry got a sentence of five years and served about four.

At first, I didn't even know that he had gone to prison. It's just not something people talk about, even inside a family. When I did find out, it was extremely difficult to accept. I was like, "Oh my God, here we go again," because a nephew of mine had gone to prison before. It's traumatizing. But it's always the same thing: no fathers in the lives of the young men, and the drugs are out there, and there's only so much you can handle in life. Perry needed his father. He never got the validation of love and respect that a boy, later a young man, needs from his father, and I think he was constantly searching for something to replace that void.

Several years after Perry got out of prison, my sister called and said that Perry was coming to Minnesota to a drug treatment program. He was coming to get himself together. He would actually get a place to live, treatment, a job, an income, a fresh start. I was excited, of course, because I was a chemical dependency nurse, so I knew I could be a good sounding board for him. I've never struggled with chemical dependency, but I know the medical side of detox. My only fear was that I wouldn't be able to help him.

He came to Minneapolis and started in the treatment program, and we talked all the time. And thank you, God, he was doing well. He was working two jobs and really trying to get his life going again. He would start his first job, at the Salvation Army, in the morning and finish his second job, as a bouncer at a bar, late at night. So I would tell him, "Don't go out of your way to do anything for me. Just focus on your sobriety."

When people go into a treatment program, in the beginning, it's best for loved ones to just stay away and let them get into a routine and work things out for themselves. I told Perry, "We can talk, and we can do things, but I don't want to be a distraction. You just need to be focused on your recovery right now. Just do your thing. We can FaceTime, but you don't need to come over and then be five minutes late for curfew at the house. You can get thrown out of the program if you violate even a simple rule."

I wanted him to finish the program before he started going out and about because he didn't have reliable transportation. And he was fine with that.

I told him that we'd have plenty of time to do things together. We were going to travel and spend time with family. I told him, "Just spend this first year focused on yourself. Get money saved. Don't worry so much about me over here. There are all types of ways to communicate if you need to."

Perry talked a lot about his mom and how much he wanted to make her happy when he completed his treatment program and had a healthy, sober lifestyle. He was focused on getting himself together and saving enough money so he could buy his mother a house. And he wanted to be a good father. He said, "I just have to make some money...the right way."

I told Perry that once he finished his program, I would try to help him get a job at the hospital where I work. He could become a mental health care technician. I told him, "We could really use someone like you, someone strong and tall to help us handle violent patients." He had experience being around all types of different people, so I thought he could be compassionate and at the same time physically strong enough to handle some of the patients when they got violent. He said he thought that would be really, really good.

Perry had my sister's heart—he was a very sweet person. And he had his father's charm and charisma. But he also had his father's demons and challenges with sobriety. He would give you the shirt off his back. At the same time, he had that pride, so he did not want to ask his family for anything. Sometimes, I would get frustrated! I would say, "Perry, you can come to me. We can talk." But Perry had that stubborn pride when things weren't going well. He wanted things to look like they were better than they were, because you're embarrassed to be a certain age and to not even be close to where you want to be in life. You want to look like you're farther along than you are. Perry used to brood about a lot of "shouldas" and "couldas," for example, that he coulda/shoulda been an NFL star, and here he was, trying to make ends meet. He was in his forties, and he wasn't getting anywhere. And that's when his mother died.

His mother, Cissy, one of my older sisters, had renal disease and a bad heart. She had been really, really sick, and in fact she had gone into hospice care. I told Perry that she was very sick, and he asked, "Should I go see her?"

I told him that he should. So he called her, and she told him not to come. She said, "I don't want you to come out of your program. You've got to stay there. If you come back, you'll fall back into this environment."

My sister lived in a part of Houston called the Third Ward. It's a neighborhood with high crime and drug use, and a difficult place to live. So his mother didn't want him to come down there and risk falling into his old habits. She told him to just stay and work it out, and that she'd be all right. Perry asked, "Are you sure?" and she said yes, so he said okay, and he didn't get to see her or say goodbye. I think that's one of the reasons he called out, "Mamma, Mamma," when he was being killed: he saw his mother, and she pulled him through to be with her again.

When Cissy passed, Perry was devastated, especially because he hadn't been able to see her and say goodbye. He was never the same. He stopped communicating with me. I tried calling him, and I tried to find him. I said that I needed to get in touch with him. The only place we would connect was at his mother's funeral. We would hug, and I would say, "Perry, just know I'm here for you." He was so sad after his mother died. I remember looking in his eyes and not seeing anything; it was just as if his eyes were dead. It was as if he were looking through me. I could see he was in trouble. I told him, "Perry, you gotta hang in there. Eventually, it will be all right. It's hard. I lost my mom. I know how you feel."

I think Perry was doubly wrecked by his mother's death because he never had a father around. He always felt like he had one parent he could count on, his mother, and he really wanted to do something special with his life and make his life a success before she left this world. I told him that his mother knew he was trying to be a better person, that he was getting clean, that he was working, that he was staying away from drugs. But I could not get him to see that.

Once I stopped hearing from him, I knew he was out there struggling somewhere. I would just pray that he had not relapsed. I would tell myself, "Maybe he's working; maybe he just doesn't want to be around people. Maybe he just needs to get himself together." But I have worked in chemical dependency too long to believe that. My instinct told me that he relapsed and that he was lost somewhere. I didn't know how to reach him. He wouldn't return calls. He wouldn't FaceTime. And his sister couldn't tell me anything—I heard the family wasn't hearing from him either. I just prayed that everything would be okay when he came out of his depression. The next time I saw Perry was when he was on that hot sidewalk with that officer's knee on his neck, and he couldn't breathe.

Perry didn't just lose his mother. He also lost his aunt's husband, Melvin Stevens. These two family members in Perry's life died a day apart. It was a really hard time for all of us; there were two funerals a few months apart. For the next two years, he was out of touch with the rest of us, in and out of trouble. He just vanished from our lives.

I don't want to make excuses for anyone's crimes. Perry did things he was not proud of. The problem is that when a person of color is found with drugs, he's just criminalized. Authorities don't associate the disease of addiction with that person. When it's a white person, and I know this is true from all my years working in chemical dependency, the first thought that comes to everybody's mind is that he is an addict. White people who get involved with drugs are addicts, but Black people who get involved with drugs are criminals. That's just how the system works.

When Perry was found with that twenty-dollar bill, which we don't even know was fake, that was no reason for him not to get help. If they thought he was on drugs, the police could have taken him somewhere for treatment. They didn't have to kneel on his neck and kill him. Tell me it wasn't because he was Black. It's just part of the systemic racism in our country, which needs to be dismantled. And that's the part that is so frustrating.

Here's an example: after Perry's death, I found out that the assistant district attorney who had prosecuted Perry on the armed robbery charge and put him in prison for four years was crooked. He had been prosecuting cases illegally, putting more charges on people than they should have gotten, and really ruining their lives. That's the prosecutor who helped convict my nephew! But when you're Black and you don't have any money, you don't have a chance in hell in the legal system.

Besides the video of Perry's murder, during the trial we saw what I guess was security video from the store, Cup Foods, where Perry supposedly passed the counterfeit bill. It showed Perry doing this little dance. When I saw it, it made me smile because he was known in the family for always clowning like that. That was the Perry we knew and loved. Then I thought, "Oh, my God, he has no idea that that's going to be the last dance he ever dances." It was the last time he talked to the folks in the store. The last time he walked out that door. The last happy moments I saw before his life ended. I wish I could have gone back in time and called Cup Foods that night. I would have asked the clerk to put Perry on the line and said to him, "Don't take that twenty-dollar bill. Just leave the store."

I remember working that day, May 25, 2020, even though it was Memorial Day. I left work and just walked, thinking it was a good day. I wasn't even tired because it hadn't been hectic at the center. I just kept walking, thinking about how I was glad to do the work I was doing, glad it was nice out. But I also remember looking up at that blue sky and thinking, "I'm glad this day is over." And then I thought, "Isn't that a weird thing to think on such a nice day?"

When I came home from work that Monday night, I didn't turn on the TV as I usually do. I just sat for a while and went to bed. The next day I learned what happened, and since then, my life has been a whirlwind.

I found out about Perry's death through the news media the next morning. I got a call from a reporter, who said he wanted to get my response to the murder of George Floyd. I said, "I don't know what you're talking about; you must have the wrong family." The reporter said, "Are you Angela Harrelson?" I said, "Well, yes, I am." And the reporter said, "Well, your nephew George was murdered by the Minneapolis police, and I would like to hear your take on it." I said, "I don't know anything about that. I think you've got the wrong family."

I didn't think it was a scam because the reporter sounded so serious. But I just walked around the house for a few minutes, and it kept bugging me. I remember talking to my husband and saying, "Have you heard about it? Somebody died?" So he went and put the TV on, and in the meantime, I looked at my text messages. I had dozens of them. And then I checked my voicemail, and I had all these voicemails. Then my sister texted and said, "Call me ASAP." So I called, but I couldn't move. Then my brother texted me and said, "Turn on the TV."

And then I saw it.

Perry was dead. The Minneapolis police killed him.

I started to think about all those text messages and voice-mails. My husband said, "Angela, come look at this." And I went into the living room and saw Perry on that hot sidewalk saying, "I can't breathe," and I saw this man, this police officer, with his knee on Perry's neck. I was just totally shocked. And then Perry said, "Mamma, mamma." Oh, my God. I just dropped to my knees because I was in shock. I fell apart. I was actually seeing Perry dying on TV. It was a modern-day lynching.

I felt so helpless. I remember getting on the phone again. I called my brother. I called my sister. There were three-way calls. There were conference calls. Everybody was calling one another. We were all trying to be close to one another so we could figure out what was going on. We were just crying and calling one another. It was so dark. Such a nightmare. We were all like, "What just happened?"

Perry's death was a nightmare for everyone in my family. It traumatized all of us, flipped everything upside down. Nothing was the same anymore. Perry was the only close family I had in Minnesota. All the plans that Perry and I had—to spend time together, to travel, to visit his uncle—they were over. I just thought we had all the time in the world, and I took it for granted that he would always be here, even when he would disappear from time to time.

11

I knew he would come back because that's what he always did—he bounced back. But that all ended on May 25, 2020.

That day changed everything. All I could think about was where I was when it happened, what I was doing, whom I was talking to. If there was something I could have done differently, if I had been there and maybe said something, maybe things would have turned out differently. It touches your gut, feeling like there's something you could have done if you had been there.

I told one of my sisters that I felt so guilty because I should have been there for him. I had served my country in the armed forces. I swore to protect and serve as a nurse. I became a first responder. But that one time, when Perry was killed, I was not there. I don't know what I would have done, but at least I could have done something. That's what I regret. Because I always thought he would come back.

All the people who saw the video recording of Perry's death saw someone die before their eyes. If you have a heart that beats and pumps the blood through your veins, that video can't do anything but change you. White, Black, red, purple, wherever you come from, you know the way he was killed, the fact that he was killed, was wrong. People told me they wanted to reach through the TV to save him. It didn't matter whether Perry had medical conditions or was on drugs. Nobody has the right to do that to any human being. Dogs get treated better than that.

I watched Derek Chauvin put his knee on my nephew's neck, applying more pressure, keeping his hands on his hips. His face and body language were like, "I've got you; what are you going to do about it?" He acted as if he had just won a trophy or gone out hunting and shot a deer. When Perry said, "I can't breathe," he was pleading with Chauvin for help. People's tax money was being spent for Chauvin to help protect them, to save lives. I'm a registered nurse, so I know about saving lives and protecting lives. But Derek Chauvin's intent was to kill. I could see it on his face.

If I had been there, if I had seen Perry on the ground with the officer's knee on his neck, if I had heard Perry begging for his life, I probably would have died too. Derek Chauvin or one of the other officers would have shot me because I would have lunged forward and tried to pull that man off my nephew's neck. There is no way, as a veteran, as a nurse, as a first responder, as an aunt, that I would have allowed that man to kill Perry.

I only saw that video one time, and I can't watch it again.

I debated whether to return to work right away. I had to get out of the house to take my mind off it all for a little while. At least I could put this energy into helping others and not dwell on Perry's death. It was much harder than I thought. I questioned myself about going to my job. What are my coworkers going to say? Will I be able to handle all the questions? I knew there was no way I would get the answers unless I tried, and that is what I decided to do.

I negotiated with myself about this decision because I did not know if I was strong enough to face the world. My emotions were all over the place, and the biggest one I carried at the time was guilt over not being there to help Perry. I was seriously asking myself, "What will I do if I get stopped by a police officer?" My emotional wounds were fresh and still painful. "If I meet a police officer, will I be able to hold it together knowing what just happened to my nephew?" I never had to find out. I had learned to stay calm and do everything the police tell you to do. Do not make sudden movements if you want to stay alive. I have been doing that for more than forty years. Having said that, I do not know if I could have held it together if I had been stopped by the police during the first year after Perry's death.

This uncertainty in my head made leaving my house to go to work a complicated question. I did not know what to expect when I got there. Yes, what happened to Perry was tragic, but there are evil people in this world who believed Perry deserved to die. "Will I encounter some of these people at work? What will I do?" The answer always came back to how God allowed me to witness a greater love than I had ever known. When I think about that love, it pushed me in a direction to go forward in love, so I did.

My familiar routine became unfamiliar to me. I could not find anything; nothing was in place. I looked for my badge, and I could not find it. I had even misplaced my job's panic button. As I got ready to open the door, I remembered. There they were, my keys, badge, and panic button right in front of me, on the table in the bedroom. The minute I got outside, I ran as fast as I could to my car. I just wanted to get in my car as quickly as possible. I did not want to meet or talk to anyone because of this fear of the unknown. I just wanted to get inside my car. My goal was to make it to work, and that's what I did.

When I look back on that frenzied morning, I realize that I was having a panic attack.

When I arrived at the nurses' station, I saw a young lady, and she told me about a video of a Black man begging for his life. She told me the police killed him, and I knew right away it was Perry. She was so shaken up that she could barely talk to me about it. When I told her that was my nephew, she suddenly paused and poured out her heart to me. I remember her telling me, "I don't want to even talk about it; it's just too painful." She said she was sorry. She was so broken, and little did she know I was barely hanging on myself. In that moment, I quickly realized that there was nowhere for me to go. People were not going to stop talking about George Floyd. This became surreal; listening to and hearing people talk about my nephew was like an out-of-body experience. Even my patients were watching TV and talking about it. Only by the grace of God did I make it through my shift that day.

When I got ready to leave my job for home, I wanted to drive by Perry's memorial, but I was told the street was closed off and it was not safe for me. I got home and turned on the TV. There, I saw millions of protesters across the world, buildings engulfed with fire, people yelling, screaming for justice. I said to myself, "Oh, my Lord—they are doing this for Perry." I didn't see them as rioters; I saw brave souls willing to risk their lives because of this injustice. Even though there was a pandemic going on, Covid had taken a back seat. People gave up their time, jobs, money to fight for this overdue cause, and I am eternally grateful.

I listened to protesters yell the words, "Say his name: GEORGE FLOYD!" and I was moved to tears when they said it because I could feel the passion, love, and conviction they expressed. Even though I was home, I said it too. I stood up in my living room, and every time people called, "Say his name!" I shouted, "GEORGE FLOYD!" I just wished he were alive to answer.

It was difficult to realize that I no longer had the option to call Perry or go to see him. That left me with a huge void in my heart and mind, and in that empty space, I had to deal with all the chaos and confusion that arrived in the aftermath of Perry's murder. I was left with questions that only I could answer: Where do I go from here? How do I deal with the press? Whom do I trust? Who will help me? Can I do it alone? I couldn't answer any of these questions at the time. I had to trust God.

About the second or third day after Perry's death, there continued to be more confusion, pain, trauma, and frustration within the hearts of the protesters. I do not blame the protesters on how they felt. There is enormous emotional pain derived from trauma pent up inside Black America after decades fighting to be free, fighting to be equal to white America.

When events settled down a little bit that first week, I visited the memorial alone. I had been there with family, but I wanted to go alone because I knew that soon my relatives would leave Minneapolis and go back to their faraway homes. I needed to be strong by myself and for myself.

Still, my mind was exhausted thinking about it all, so much so that I often felt numb inside. How could this be allowed to happen to a Black man again and again in the twenty-first century? I played the video over and over in my mind. It all came back to the fact that he was murdered by a police officer because he was Black and poor, had a prior record, and was seen as less than a human being.

Meanwhile, people were planning all kinds of memorials and events about his murder, and the legal machinery started up with the district attorney's office to decide on charges for the officers involved. Things were moving really fast. Right away, there were protests here in the Twin Cities, then other places in Minnesota, then all over the country, and even outside the United States. I started hearing about rallies in Germany and London, white people protesting Perry's murder. I felt overwhelming waves of love coming from unexpected places.

All these things happened so fast. One memorial after another. I went to so many of them. My body was moving fast, my mind was moving fast—no time to take a breather. People forget that you haven't had time to grieve. I never had time to grieve that first year. A year after Perry's death, I still have spells of crying. It's like it happened just yesterday. When I walk around Minneapolis today, Perry's face is everywhere. He's on the wall in the square where he was killed. It's on hundreds of placards people hold at rallies. I go to the store, and his face is there. But Perry isn't here. I'm still dealing with that.

Some people paint Perry as if he were stone evil. He did some bad things, as I've said, but a lot of God-fearing people make some very bad decisions. This doesn't make them evil. There were people who told me that Perry deserved to die. That broke my heart; it brought me to tears. Perry was sweet, but it doesn't matter what kind of person you are, how often you go to church, or what you believe when the drugs take hold of you. This is true regardless of race or religion. That's the only positive thing you can say about drugs: they don't discriminate! White or Black, you're going down!

The authorities just wanted to call Perry a drug addict and a criminal. But his life still had value. He had kids. He had a family that loved him, and his life was just as valuable as anybody else's. My job now is to make sure that Perry's death was not in vain. It gives me peace to know that his death opened up transparency to the ugly racism that has existed in this country for four hundred years because people still don't believe us.

As days went by, a spiritual message grew in my mind. Perry showed bravery in the last few minutes of his life. He was fighting to live with his words. Somehow, under those awful conditions, barely hanging on, Perry was able to muster the words, "I can't breathe" and "Mamma, mamma." The message I received was that if Perry could find the strength to try to save his own life while a police officer killed him, then I could find the strength to become a voice for him. I could be a motivator to people to fight for racial justice, and that could be part of Perry's legacy.

This book is necessary because so many people don't know the whole story. I was at some evening event, and I heard one white person say to another, "What is there to say about George Floyd?

He's a guy who did bad things, and he got killed." I told that man that there was a lot to say about George Floyd because there is so much more to his story and so much that people don't know about him. I told them how he couldn't go back to Houston when his mother was dying and didn't get to say goodbye to her, and how heartbroken he was. Once people listen to the other side of the story, it's really eye-opening for them; it changes their perceptions when they have more information. I didn't intend to make a speech, but within about five minutes, there were about fifteen or twenty people in front of me, engrossed in our conversation. They were riveted by what I was saying because they hadn't heard it on TV or social media, and they were hungry to learn more.

People got to see the ugly truth of racism with Perry's murder, and they can't hide from it anymore. It's opened up a conversation. Racism never got talked about outside the Black community. Now a lot of white people are trying to take racism seriously; they're no longer in denial about it, and they're trying to stand up for us.

It's gut-wrenching for me to relive these experiences, but people need to know the story. People need to know Perry's story, and my story, which is not very different from the experiences of most Black Americans. So let me tell you how we grew up.

CHAPTER 2

"This Is the White Train, Not the Soul Train": Growing Up in the Racist South

I grew up in a town called Goldsboro, North Carolina. We didn't have *anything*. My mother, bless her heart, wanted the best for us. She worked in those tobacco fields and cornfields to make sure we had what we needed. My father became a cook, but he always had to enter the restaurants where he worked from the back. That's what Black people had to do.

Goldsboro was a small town controlled by whites, but it had a big population of Black folks. We saw white people a lot because we worked on their farms. My parents were sharecroppers who didn't have much money and weren't educated people. My mamma gave birth to fourteen kids. I was born in 1962 with a fraternal twin sister, Mahalia Jones, who my mother named after the famous gospel singer, Mahalia Jackson. If you worked on the land and lived in a house that belonged to the landowner, you had better not stop working. If you did, they'd kick you out of the house. Not only did you not own the house, you didn't own much of anything inside the house. As we got older, we had to work in the fields to help buy our school clothes.

As children, we had to walk up this long path to catch the school bus because no bus would go that far deep into the woods to pick us up. This was in the late 1960s and the early 1970s, and the schools had just recently integrated. People were still getting used to the idea of integration. It hadn't just happened—it had been going on for a few years. But the South hadn't gotten used to it. North Carolina was slow at getting it done.

When I started school, I automatically felt that as a Black child, I was treated as less intelligent than the white kids. My mom tried to prepare me for this treatment by raising us to be submissive to them, hoping that would help her kids succeed. In grade school, I was noticeably quiet and did not say much in class. I did my work well, and my grades were exceptionally good. The teacher did not understand my quietness and shyness, which came from being around a lot of white kids for the first time. The teacher was the first white female authority figure I experienced up close, and I was intimidated by her presence. There were a handful of other Black kids at the school, and I am not sure how they were treated, but I don't think it was much better.

On the first day of first grade, my teacher asked me my name. I told her it was Angela Jones. She said, "Well, your middle name is Terry." I said, "Yes, it is, but my momma calls me Angela." The teacher said, "Well, Angela, your name is going to be Terry because it will be easier for you to spell than Angela." I was too afraid to say anything, and I wanted to cry because I wanted to be called the name that my mother called me at home. I never told my mom because I didn't think she could help me contradict a white teacher. It was not until much later, in high school, that I found the courage to ask the teachers to call me Angela.

Even early in childhood, we lived in fear of what we faced at school. One day, the teacher had to leave the room for some reason, so she turned to one of the white students and said, "You go stand up front by the chalkboard and just make sure that everybody behaves, and if anybody misbehaves, write their name down on the chalkboard."

I was too scared to breathe because no one who looked like me was anywhere near me. There were only two or three Black children in the class, and the teacher made us sit far apart. I didn't have the comfort of my twin sister because she was put in another class.

All I could think about was not making the slightest sound. It was like a nightmare: don't make a sound or the monster will get you. But I must have accidentally jogged my pencil because it rolled off my desk. It was so quiet in the classroom that when the pencil hit the floor, it sounded like a bomb going off.

The white girl pounced. "You did it!" she shouted at me. "I'm writing your name down! You're in trouble!"

All the other students were looking at me like I'd done something awful. I was terrified. All because a pencil rolled down my desk. The teacher came back and saw my name. I didn't say anything because I had been raised not to say anything in these situations. I was so scared.

As punishment for making noise in class, the teacher assigned me homework of writing some sentence a hundred times. It was really hard for me because I was in first grade and hadn't learned how to write! That's how things were back then. By the time I finished, I was thinking, "Maybe I *did* do something wrong!"

My mother raised us to be obedient to white people and always do what the white people said so we wouldn't get in trouble. When I went home, hurt and confused, I didn't even want to tell my mother I had gotten in trouble, but somehow she knew. I was scared that she would be upset with me too, but I told her what had happened, and I cried. Momma just shook her head and said, "You could have yawned, and you still would have gotten in trouble because you're Black. It'll be all right."

This is the kind of experience that most white children never have in school, and when they witness a Black person going through it, they don't think about it as something wrong because it isn't happening to them. It's just part of the way things are.

Because my mother raised me to be submissive to white people, I never questioned them. I was not sure how to interact with them because I did not know how to navigate in that environment. After school, I played on my tire swing and danced with my twin sister almost every day. The next day at school, I was extremely quiet again. I did not know what to say and frankly, I felt inferior to the white children and the teacher.

Even though my grades were good, the teacher told my mom that I had to repeat the first grade because I didn't talk in class; I was too quiet. I told my mom that it wasn't right, I was doing fine in school, and I showed her all my papers with stars on them. My mom said, "The teacher says you do not talk in class; you are too quiet." She said I'd be fine going through first grade a second time—I just needed to talk more. My mother knew what the teacher did was wrong, but she did not have the courage to go against a white teacher's decision. The school held back my sister Mahalia too! We both had to repeat first grade.

As I kept going up in grades and got used to school cultures, I became better about speaking in class. I got accustomed to seeing different races and learned how to adapt. If only that teacher had taken a little more time with me, she would have known I was a normal kid who was just shy.

In another school year, I remember this white boy talking bad about Black people in the classroom. He was carrying on how Blacks were not as smart as white people. He looked at me and said, "If they were smart, why hasn't there ever been a Black president?" The teacher heard it all. I did not say anything in the class. The teacher easily could have asked him to stop and said, "Because there isn't one now, there is always a chance it can happen if they study and work hard." But she didn't correct the boy or scold him for saying something bad about Black people. The job of the teacher is to encourage students and say that everyone has the chance to succeed. When Obama became president, I wondered if that boy was still living and whether he'd had a change of heart.

One day, when I was around twelve and my mother was walking us to the bus, the bus just kept going. The white kids stuck their hands out of the windows and waved, yelling, "Bye, n-----s, bye!" We just stood there watching it go. The next day, we went out to the bus again. This time, they had signs on the bus that said *white only*. I remember the driver rolling down the window and shouting, "This is the white train, not the *Soul Train*." That got my mother really upset. She said, "You're going to school. You're going to get that high school diploma." My father had to go to the school and argue with the principal to get us on the school bus, which was our legal right.

We had the right to ride the bus, but riding to school was a miserable experience. As soon as we got on the school bus, white kids threw trash at us. They called us names. They put their feet on the seats and wouldn't let us sit down. So we had to stand, and the bus driver would drive around the corners really, really fast. We would accidentally fall on the white children, and then we would get in trouble.

One day, one of my friends, a boy named James, accidentally bumped into a white kid because the bus driver intentionally took a turn too fast. He held on as tight as he could, but he couldn't fight the sway of the bus when the driver roared around that corner. James barely touched the white boy, but the kid stood up and slapped James as hard as he could with his open hand. We Black kids should have stood up for James, but we didn't. I froze in my tracks and didn't move. All I did was watch the tears roll down James's face and feel terrible because I couldn't help him.

The driver actually named his dog N----r—somehow all the kids knew that—and he would incite the white kids to get violent with us. He would say things like, "If any of the n-----r kids say anything, you have to hit them!" At one point, my twin sister Mahalia, who was a fighter, said something. Two boys hit her. One looked as if he didn't want to do it but knew he had to because the bus driver said so. The other one? Well, let's just say that Mahalia was a fighter and she fought back. She *really* fought back. She got the best of that white boy, believe me.

The amazing thing is, many years later, the bus driver and Mahalia were in a store and they recognized each other! The bus driver actually apologized to her, which was something that would never have happened back then. And then, here's the best part. He said to her, "You sure beat the hell out of that white kid!"

I remember when we came home from school, we'd get off the school bus and they would throw more trash at us. This went on for at least a couple of months. Then we told our mother that we didn't want to take that school bus anymore. And you know what she told us? "You're going to take that school bus, and you're going to graduate from high school because I didn't. And you're going to fight." And I'm like, "How are we supposed to beat all those white people?"

The next day, my mother walked us up to the bus stop, and she made us get on the bus. I remember that day so well. I looked back at her, and her hands were on her hips and she nodded her head as if to say, "You're getting on that bus."

I was thinking, "Oh my God, how I just dread this."

But we got on that school bus. And of course the driver was still saying, "This is the white train, not the *Soul Train!*" We headed for the back because the white kids still wouldn't let us sit in any of the seats up front, and, as I said, we couldn't sit down in the back because they would put their feet on the seats. But there was a white girl around my age, and she stood up on that bus and she shouted, "My mamma said, 'You don't treat them like that.'"

She said it so loud you could hear a pin drop afterward. That was a white girl talking!

Next thing I knew, feet began to move off the seats. People got up and let us sit down. And I'm thinking, "All that, just so that we could ride a school bus." Because a little girl had the courage to speak up, we were able to sit down.

I thought about that girl and what she did for us when I saw the video of my nephew lying there for those nine minutes. There were people around him who were experienced, who had wisdom, who were adults, and they couldn't even do that—they couldn't even say what she said. But that moment on the bus changed my outlook on life. I began to believe that there were people who cared.

We were so happy when we came home from school. We said, "Mamma, we didn't have to fight!" And she said, "Y'all are good." Our mother was so happy. From that day forward, we got on the school bus, we just sat down, and we just stayed quiet. We didn't cause any trouble. We were happy to just sit down on the bus, to ride the bus to school and come home.

The white kids didn't really say anything to us after that. They just kept to themselves. They didn't make friends with us. But that one girl who had spoken up did say, "Hi, how y'all doing?" Things like that. We would just say, "We're doing fine," and then we would stay quiet. We were just those kids who had been raised up old-school. You sit down, you be quiet, you don't say too much. And that's what we did every day.

My mother had little education; she had to drop out of school at thirteen and raise kids. Because of that, she was determined that all her children would earn high school diplomas.

When we did, she acted as if we'd won gold medals—and she had too. She didn't think in terms of college for us. It wasn't part of her vision for her children. She may have been trying to protect us from disappointment. But several of us did go to college and earn degrees, and she was very proud of us.

One thing my mother knew was our family history, and she always made sure we knew about it. My great-grandfather, Hillary Thomas Stewart Senior, who was born a slave and was freed when he was eight years old, bought his first land when he was twenty-one. Over the years, he developed about five hundred acres of land, but it was stolen from him. Mamma said the white men stole it from him because he couldn't read and didn't know how to calculate the taxes—he didn't have all the knowledge he needed. And she said the white people stole all our land. She never let us forget that. Although he couldn't read, my great-grandfather took pains to uncover his family history and teach his son, my grandfather, about it. My grandfather passed along the history to my mother, who shared it with all her children.

My mother raised us to be careful. She raised us always to address white people by their last name, not by their first name. She always said, "Never enter the house of a white person from the front door; always enter from the back. Don't sit in the front rows of a bus; sit in the back. Don't sit in the front seat of a white person's car; always get in the back if you have to get in their car. If a white person is walking on the sidewalk and you're walking on the sidewalk in the other direction, step into the street so the white person has the sidewalk to herself." My mother was very passive about racial matters because that's how she was raised. She thought she was doing the right thing, of course, but little did she know she was passing on the message they taught people down South: if you're Black, stay in your place.

We already felt different because we were so poor. We didn't have anything. We had no money. We were the kids who lived far back in the woods. We already felt out of place, that we were never good enough, because that's how most of the white folks treated us. We were taught by word and by example that white people had a superior status to ours, which made us feel inferior. When we saw white people, we knew they weren't our equals; they were better than we were. They deserved more because they were white.

As a child growing up, that made me feel inferior. If something went wrong and a white person was to blame, you knew it was going to be your fault anyway. That's how I grew up, and that's how I felt until I knew better. Luckily, my mother also told us we could achieve great things as adults. She said, "You may have to work twice as hard because you are Black, but you can do it."

The layers run so deep in systemic racism. My great-grandfather and my grandfather lived in those layers, and the exploitation passed down to my mother. Everything that has happened and everything we've talked about since Perry died bring me back to my mom and her tears of distress when things went wrong simply because we were Black people living in a world controlled by whites. White civic leaders did everything to continue to exploit us as though we were not human beings, they convinced thousands of Black Americans that their lives were not as valuable as the lives of white people, and they silenced our voices on the street and at the ballot box.

It was Perry's mom, my sister Cissy, who told me the most about how we Black folks were being exploited. She knew things way before I did because she was one of the older siblings, and my momma would confide in her.

Probably the lowest episode Momma experienced was when she was still young, before I was born. She had a total of ten girls and four boys, but Frank Jones was her son who died. He was probably less than six months old. My dad and mother were still working on the farm as sharecroppers, not having much money and stuff. My father hated being a sharecropper, and he had got into a terrible argument with the white farmer who owned the land. He refused to do any more work for him. The man had called him a nigger, and it triggered an emotion that my father had never experienced before, and it made him argue even more with the landowner. It was really cold that day, and the white man told him to get out—"I want you out of the house, off my land."

My mom tried to pack what she could, and she covered up baby Frank as best she could and wrapped him against her body. They didn't have a car, and they had to walk far up the road to her grandparents' house, and the baby caught a cold and got very sick. My mother was distraught because she felt like the man didn't show any compassion. She was mad at my father, but she was angrier at the white man who put them out. The baby died because he had caught pneumonia, and my mother blamed the white farmer. My mother never got over the death of losing that baby.

It wasn't all sadness. As I mentioned before, my mother had a gift for playing piano; she'd been playing since she was four years old. Even when things were rough, there was music around the house, and playing would make her happy. People from miles around would hear her playing our old piano, and often they would follow the music and come to the house to hear Momma play. She'd play a lot of gospel music, like "This Little Light of Mine" and "Amazing Grace" recorded by Mahalia Jackson. At Christmastime, her favorite was "Silent Night."

Momma worked in the chicken house and the tobacco fields all her life. When she was getting older, and she couldn't work like she used to, one day she went down to the Social Security office to see what she and my dad would collect after they retired. When she came home, she was very sad, her head hanging down. I finally got up the nerve to ask her what was wrong, and all she said was, "Get your education, make sure you get your high school diploma. I want you to be better than I am."

Later, Cissy told me that Momma was sad because there may not be much to collect from Social Security when she got older. They were told there was hardly any money in there because nothing had ever been paid into the Social Security system from their paychecks. My parents weren't educated; they didn't understand how Social Security worked. They just knew they worked, and people paid them money, and they cashed the check at the store the landowners told them to go to. She must have said something about it, because one day the farmers' accountant came to the house, the gentleman who kept the books for the landowners. Cissy told me after the meeting that this man had told my mother that if she said anything else about Social Security, we would have to move out of our house.

That's why my mom was so fearful, afraid to go to Social Security or any other government office to fight, because she had had that trauma: she was so devastated by the death of her baby son. When you're powerless, when you don't have any money, when you know that the white people just control everything, you accept things the way they are.

I thought about that conversation with Cissy when Perry died. I realized that my parents' inability to get some Social Security and the accountant's threat were part of a racist system that reached into the lives of almost every Black person. I started reading and reading about systemic racism and how it worked because I knew I'd be doing a lot of public speaking, and I wanted to back up what I said with the scholarship of people who had studied systemic racism.

What stood out to me in all this reading was how powerful systemic racism is and for how long it's been going on, has been brewing and working in white supremacy for years. I said to myself, "My God, white people have been getting away with this for years." Everybody acts as if systemic racism began yesterday, but it is nothing new. It's been around for centuries, just called different things. There was slavery, then there was peonage, which is when someone pays off a debt by working at something against their will. Sharecropping is just one form of peonage. So is forcing an immigrant to work off passage to the United States by working in a sweatshop or as a prostitute. Forcing someone into peonage is illegal, but it happens all the time.

Eventually my momma was able to qualify for disability from Social Security, and my father took a job at a barbecue pit where the boss didn't pay him much, but he did take out the Social Security tax. If not for that, we probably would have had to support Momma for years after she stopped working. This is how it is when you're uneducated: you just want to survive, and the system throws obstacles in your way. Momma didn't want trouble because she feared the white man. They had the power, and she was afraid.

But she had a lot of hope for my generation. Even though she communicated to us that we should try to avoid racism rather than fight it, she wanted all of us to try to finish high school and to make something of ourselves in the white world. She wanted us to travel, to see the world, to do a lot of the things she didn't get to do because she got pregnant so young and had so many kids. All her life was spent raising kids and working, and even though she didn't want us to have the life she had, her life was an inspiration to me.

Each one of us had a unique bond with Momma because many of us worked side by side with her in the tobacco fields. It was hard work in the hot sun: Momma would wear a big hat to keep the sun off her face, and we would have scarves tied around our heads to hold the sweat. She would tell me about things that happened in her life, and I would be intrigued by her stories and listen hard. Her way of showing love was to sweat and work hard to put food on the table, and I understood that.

Sometimes my mother would be out there with a toothache and pain shooting through her back, but she would keep right on going. I honestly don't know how she did it. It was pure love and desire to have the best for your kids. She taught us that life is hard, but we Blacks are a resilient race and need to keep faith that if we keep on going, the next generation will have things better.

If Momma were here, she would be distraught over what happened to her grandson. But she was also a praying woman, and she would hold on to her faith that everything would be okay. Not one day goes by that I don't think about Perry or about my mom. The thoughts of them go hand in hand. I think of her when I need a mother; when I do, her spirit is right here, and I can talk to her.

Sometimes I ask, "Mom, how am I going to get through this? What am I going to do?" Then I think about what she did to get through all her problems because her life was much tougher than mine, but she just kept hanging in there. She reminds me that I will get through whatever I'm facing and be okay.

I made the cheerleading squad in high school when there weren't but two or three Black girls on the squad. I got on because, sure enough, I worked twice as hard and was twice as good as the white girls. It's still that way for Black people. The white cheerleaders didn't give us any trouble, didn't freeze us out in practice or on the field, but we knew our place. We knew that after practice or a game, we wouldn't be hanging out with them. The Black cheerleaders were the ones that I could hang with and feel comfortable with.

It wasn't cool for white kids to hang out with Black kids where I grew up. The white girls on the squad would have been a little ashamed of being seen socially with Black girls, even if they were fellow cheerleaders. It would have been a downgrade for them. That made me feel bad because I wanted to be friends with all the girls on the squad. They were friend*ly* enough: they'd talk to me and laugh with me, but back then, no white girl was going to invite me home to dinner.

That understanding followed me into adult life—into the military, into college, into the workplace. I wouldn't be hostile to white people, I'd treat them fine, but I knew that if I made friends with a white person, sooner or later she wouldn't be my friend anymore. That attitude, which carried over from my high school years, kept me from getting close to people who might have made wonderful friends. I wanted to head off that feeling of being not good enough to socialize with white people, so I kept them at arm's length.

My heart breaks when I see or read about a Black kid who is the only Black student in a gifted class or a music academy or given an internship at a large corporation because that youngster is basically a token. Not only is that person unlikely to socialize with the white kids in the class or the office, but if something goes wrong, the powers that be will look at him first as the person who made the error or committed a lapse in judgment.

I can barely remember a time when I didn't feel different because I was Black. Even before I started school and was around people all day who didn't look like me, I knew. I knew because my mother was always submissive and extra humble in front of white people, and she was teaching me to be the same way because she thought it would protect me. And, let's be honest, she did not want me to get in trouble that would lead to us getting kicked off the land we farmed and out of our house, the biggest fear for sharecroppers. The only way we could stay in that ratty old house was by staying and working on that land. Having to be extra polite and humble in front of white people was when I knew the most that I was different from them.

I left Goldsboro in the early 1980s when an older sister, Laura Stevens, asked me if I would move to Iowa, where she had moved. I said sure. I took the bus and I was scared to death! I rode that thing all the way to Iowa. And that's where I lived with my sister in Cedar Rapids, which was shocking to me because everybody around me was white. Even though it was supposed to be better up North, the difference is that the whites down South were open about their racism. They'll call you the n-word to your face. In the North, it was all done behind your back. I didn't like that at all!

I was around twenty when I moved, and I wanted to go to nursing school. I tried to apply, but they said they wouldn't take me because I was Black. They were pretty up-front about it. The nursing instructor told me that she didn't think I could be a nurse. I asked why. She said, "You don't have all the math courses. All you have is high school, and you shouldn't even try to apply because you don't have the requirements." I said, "Well, I can get the requirements. I just need a chance." And she said no.

I got discouraged, but I wasn't going to quit. I thought, "I may not be able to go to nursing school, but let me go to community college. Let me do something." So I joined the military. I joined the Army National Guard, and at the same time I went to Kirkwood Community College in Iowa. I was so excited because now I was going to get the requirements taken care of to become a nurse. I was thinking about maybe going to law school.

But then I ran into racism again. I wanted to take a course on bankruptcy law. The professor called me into his office and asked, "Why are you taking this course?" Now remember, this isn't the 1950s—it's the mid-1980s! I told him I wanted to be a nurse, but I wanted to take some courses in law in case I decided to go to law school.

He said, "Let me tell you something. You need to drop out of this program. I am a racist, and I don't teach Black people who want to pursue law." He said that right to my face! It was humiliating and it intimidated me as well.

Nevertheless, I hung in there and got my two-year degree in psychology, and then I went to Mount Mercy College and got a bachelor's degree in psychology. And then I went back and picked up another degree in nursing. I just kept going. Even though people told me that I couldn't do it, I just kept trying. And through it all, I became a captain in the Air Force Reserve.

If you're not a strong person, you'll give up. But I'll tell you what made me strong. It was working in those tobacco fields when I was ten or eleven years old. We would be all muddy, but it didn't matter. You had no choice. There were no babysitters. Everybody looked after one another. I remember walking down the tobacco rows right alongside my mother. She was trying to show me how to pull weeds out of the tobacco. And I would look at her and see her with all that wet stuff coming down her face. She was so hot, and she had that big straw hat on. She knew I was getting thirsty, so she would stop to get me water. She would say, "We got to keep going. We'll make it to the end. And then we can sit down and rest." That's how I had the strength to carry on.

We were probably making just $1.50 an hour back then, but she wanted the best for her kids. And I remember crying. I wanted to make sure I did better in life so my mother could be proud of me, so that she would not feel as though her life was for nothing.

I was in the Army National Guard for about ten years. My mother was so proud of me. There was racism in the Army as well. I was trying to take the officer test, and a major told me, "Don't even waste your time taking that test. You're never going to be able to score high." I remember wanting to cry. I had just graduated from college. I had a four-year degree. But he still said, "Don't waste your time. You're not smart enough. You're never going to do it." I knew that he was telling me that because I was Black. In the eighties, it was very hard to be a Black female officer in the Army, so I just let it go and kept trying. I took the test, and later I found out that my test scores had been changed. But I just kept pursuing the dream to be an officer in the military. I just could not let go of that image of my mother pushing through the tobacco rows. I just remember that I had to push through.

When I was in Officer Training School, I saw other Black women. I saw white women, Black men, everybody. I saw doctors. I saw attorneys. We were all studying together. And that was just a weird feeling because I was sitting there with these attorneys and doctors, colonels, all these people, and I was thinking about how proud I felt because I had worked so hard to get there. All the racism, the people changing my test scores, telling me, "No, you can't." It took me longer than other people, perhaps, but it was sweet when I got there.

I became a mental health nurse in the Air Force Guard and Reserve when I moved to Minneapolis to take a commission in the Air Force. Three years into my officer career, 9/11 happened. It was a scary time, but I survived it. Minnesota is a predominantly white state, of course. Are people racist here? You would be surprised. Everybody talks about "Minnesota nice," but there's another side to things here. I'll give you an example. I went to a beautician here in Minneapolis, and all I wanted was to get my hair washed. And she said, "I can't do that. I can't help you." I explained all I wanted was just to get my hair washed and taken care of. The stylist said, "Well, I've never done Black hair before," and I said, "You are trained to know how to wash and condition anybody's hair. You can do that much for me. You don't have to put a weave in. I will pay you. I have an appointment, and I'm not going anywhere." You can call it my Rosa Parks moment! She found someone to do the washing, and she conditioned my hair, and then she admitted, "You know, I was just scared." I said, "You don't have to be scared. You just have to stop being afraid of us."

She said, "You're right." She told me it was a learning moment for her.

My husband, Vins Harrelson, and I live in an area here in Minneapolis that's mixed-race. He's a flight attendant for Delta. Our building is predominantly white, but there are many Black people too. The church I attend is mostly Black. People pretty much stay to themselves. Nobody wants to get to know anybody. I've always treated the white people in my building or in my neighborhood nicely and kindly. I know my role. I know my place. I do know that if I come home late from work, I shouldn't go in the elevator because if there are some white people in the elevator by themselves, they're afraid of me. So I take the stairs because I don't want to scare anybody. You know what I'm saying?

You might think I'm overreacting. But my experience is that if I get off late from work, around one or two in the morning, and I get in the elevator with a white woman, she will clutch her purse tightly. If white people don't know me personally, there's a good chance they'll have this stereotype about Black people. To avoid all that, I just take the stairs. I don't want any trouble. You have to do these things. Otherwise, this is how people get shot and killed. Because they're in an elevator, and a white person thinks they're being threatened. They call the police, and the next thing that happens, there's another shooting of a Black person. All because of fear and prejudice.

If somebody's mind is made up that they're afraid of Black people and you're in the elevator with them, they could pull out a gun. Or call the police. And as I said, my mother always, always raised us to be careful. But almost all Blacks think about what could happen. Not what *will* happen but what might happen because people are afraid of us. I don't want people afraid of me. I don't think I'm a scary person! But you have to be careful nonetheless.

I'll tell you another story. I used to go to the same Hallmark store every week, buying tons and tons of gifts for my family. The manager and I knew each other by first name. Usually the store closed at 10:00, but one night it closed at 9:30. I didn't know. I went in after 9:30 because the door was open. Now keep in mind I've known the manager for several years. The same white manager I had been talking to and laughing with all that time and enjoyed spending my money in his store. For the first time, I saw he was afraid of me. He backed away from me as if I'd never been in his store before. I saw this fear in his eyes because I was in there after hours. He no longer looked at me as this friendly Black person spending money. He was looking at me like, "I don't trust you anymore." You see what I'm saying? It's heartbreaking because I spent money there all that time. That taught me another lesson about being Black in America.

Let's say I'm stopped by a police officer. I tell the officer everything I'm doing. If I reach to get my wallet, I'll say first, "Mister Policeman, I'm going to take my driver's license out. Is it okay if I do that?" I do that every step of the way so I don't get killed. That's how Black people have to think. That's how we survive. White people don't realize this.

Sometimes when I go into a store, I will be followed. I'm not trying to steal anything! Maybe I just need help trying to find something! It is exhausting. It's tiring. But I do these things to be careful so I can survive. I'm always conscious. I'm Black, and I have to be careful. It can be exhausting, but it's survival.

Along the same line, if I walk out of a store, I always make sure I have my receipt in my hand. The same thing is true if I go to a gas station to buy gas. I always make sure I have my receipt. I don't drive away without a receipt in case somebody stops me and says that I didn't pay for the gas. That happened once. I had paid for the gas, and I showed the woman at the station the receipt when she challenged me. She actually looked at the date and the time on the receipt. She said that the cameras made her think that I drove off without paying for gas. That's why I take my receipt every single time.

One of the reasons I wrote this book is that when Perry moved to Minnesota, my sister asked me to keep an eye on him, look after him. I tried my best to do that, although I couldn't save him. When he was killed, I was devastated—I'm still devastated—but I felt it was my responsibility to speak out about his death, not just on behalf of Perry, but for all Black people who have died at the hands of public officials. I needed to become an active part of the effort to stop this madness of inequality.

When I look back at my life growing up with blatant racism, all of us trying to do the best we could for ourselves as kids, I realize that we didn't have control over how to narrate our stories. It's only since the modern civil rights movement began that Black people have gained opportunities—very slowly—to tell our own stories. By telling Perry's story, along with the history of my family and some of the history of Black people in America, I have a chance to narrate the story myself and tell it the way it should be told. I can help get the message out that we are human beings, that we matter, that Black Lives Matter.

No one is born a racist. It is learned behavior that can be taught or influenced by role models, parents, teacher, and leaders. I am not a psychologist about kids' racism. I can only tell you from a Black childhood growing up in schools that I was treated differently. I believe that teachers especially have a responsibility to pay attention to children's behaviors when there are kids in a class dominated by another race or culture.

Black people reading this will understand everything I'm saying. It may come as news to some Caucasians reading this, but that's another reason why I'm writing this book, so that you'll understand too! One thing white people need to understand is why the murder of my nephew changed everything for Black Americans. To put it simply, we've run out of patience. Maybe it's because Perry was killed during the Covid-19 pandemic and so many of us had lost our jobs. Who knows why it was Perry's death and not James Byrd's or Michael Brown's or Trayvon Martin's or any of the other Black men who have been killed in recent years. For whatever reason, it was Perry. And when he died, Black America had run out of patience. In the next chapter, I'll explain why.

CHAPTER 3

Why Black People Are
Out of Patience

I feel like we're the only race that has to negotiate for equality. Think about it: we've been negotiating equality for four hundred years. Negotiating to rise above where we started. Negotiating the vote. We even had to negotiate whom we could marry. We had to negotiate the right to be educated. Under slavery, it was illegal for us to get an education. Later, we went to segregated schools, and our textbooks were the ones that got too old and raggedy for the white students to use.

One of the things the owners took away from enslaved people was unity. They weren't allowed to speak their own languages. They took away the slaves' names so they could have no connection to their past. They couldn't find out where their ancestors came from, let alone enjoy any cultural legacy from them. I thank God that my great-grandfather worked hard to uncover his history and teach us who we were on his side.

We've been going through this for years in this country. First, most Black people were enslaved, and then, after slavery ended, we had to deal in the South with what they called the Black Codes, which became what we know as Jim Crow laws. Those were laws specifically meant to humiliate Black people and keep them down, keep them from living a normal daily life. Black people couldn't go out at certain times of night; they'd be suspected of crimes. If a Black man was walking around day or night because he was homeless or unemployed, he'd get thrown in jail for vagrancy. You couldn't vote unless you could pass a difficult "literacy" test. Separate water fountains. Sitting in the back of the bus. Not being served in restaurants. Some of these Jim Crow laws were so crazy that, honestly, I don't even know how we made it as far as we've come.

With the civil rights laws in the sixties, we thought things were getting better, but things really didn't get better because what the white establishment did was restructure its hate into health care systems, prison systems, school systems, judicial systems. They made it difficult for Black people to purchase homes where they wanted to because they had an agreement not to sell a Black person a house in certain neighborhoods. Judges would sentence Black people to years in jail and give white people probation for the same crime. They just restructured everything to what we today call systemic racism.

Even one hundred years after enslaved Blacks were freed, the last thing white people wanted was for Black people to get good jobs and make good livings, to own property, to attend elite schools. To this day, there's a huge wealth gap between white and Black people; the average Black person's net worth is a tiny fraction of the average white person's. Black students are under-represented at every elite college that isn't majority Black already,

That's why I think we're tired, because we've been negotiating everything about our lives for so many years. We are just tired. I didn't experience those days with the "colored only" water fountains, but we all heard about them, and all the other things Black people couldn't do, the way they had to live. We took in all the stories and carried them around with us. We had to think about them all the time. Every minute of every day, we carry the weight of our history with us.

So now we can drink at any water fountain we want, but even though the twenty-first century is an upgrade in our status, we still have to get up in the morning and think about how we have to behave. We have to think about how we need to act and what we can't do in front of white people, especially white people in authority. I had to tell Perry, when he was a young man, to be careful: "You're tall, you're six foot four. If you get stopped, the police might be a little afraid of you." You have to have that conversation. Most white mothers and aunts don't have to have that conversation with their sons and nephews. They may just say, "Drive careful, don't drink, don't text; you'll be okay."

It's that extra stuff that makes us tired. To have to give the same talk, all the time, over all the years of your life is just exhausting. That's why we say we're tired. We literally are exhausted because equality is our birthright—we are all God's children—but people don't see it that way, so we've had to fight for equality every step of the way. For most of our history in America, equality wasn't even an option. Now it is, but we still have to fight for it, for our birthright. Our problem isn't white people in general because there are white people who recognize our common humanity. Our problem is the people who don't see us as human beings. You get tired of that. That's why it is exhausting, and we don't want to do it anymore.

Some people ask, "Why did it take Perry's death to get folks angry enough to protest in the streets all over the country?" By the time Perry was killed, we had lost dozens of our people to police violence just in the past ten years. Trayvon Martin. Tamir Rice. Ahmaud Arbery. Breonna Taylor. The list goes on and on. Why did patience run out with Perry?

I think a lot of it has to do with the coronavirus pandemic, which had most Americans under stay-at-home orders in May 2020. Millions of people sat in front of their TVs for more hours than they were used to. They were in position to see a video of something most of them had never seen before—a modern-day lynching.

They saw a Black man who, for the time he was conscious, was preaching his own funeral, saying, "I can't breathe," and crying out for his mother. He knew he was going to die. In the video, they could see the pain in his face, the blood running out of his nose. It brought people to tears.

And they could see that the pain Perry was in was caused by a man with his knee on his neck, looking totally unconcerned, with his hands on his hips, not letting anyone come up and help Perry. The officer wasn't a big man, but he was strong; he knew how to apply pressure. During the trial, it came out that he shifted his weight so he could press harder on Perry's neck. And he mocked Perry. At one point, when Perry said, "I can't breathe," the officer said something like, "You must be able to breathe if you're talking."

Perry's hands were cuffed behind his back. He wasn't kicking the officer. He wasn't fighting him, he wasn't trying to run away— he wasn't even calling him names. Imagine how Perry must have felt: immobilized, in pain, scared to pieces, knowing in his heart that he was going to die. And his killer was mocking him.

I think when people saw that video again and again, the humanity factor kicked in. All kinds of people, including white people, said, "Wait a minute, this is wrong, this is not just, he's a human being, you don't do somebody that way." Something about the inhumane way Perry was treated just resonated with most of the people who saw the video. That's what moved the world: a nation of people watching that video, minute after minute, thinking, "Get off him, stop, leave him alone." It was so excruciating, so painful to watch—for everybody, not just family and not just Black folks. People from everywhere couldn't get the image of that officer's knee on Perry's neck out of their heads.

The video, and the number of people who saw it, changed everything because it wasn't about just race anymore: it was about humanity. That video lit the fuse. A lot of people who started out by yelling at their TVs, hollering, "Stop it! Get off him!" spilled out into the streets because they wanted people to understand how wrong it was that Perry was killed the way he was killed.

Perry showed so much courage in that video. It took all his strength just to say, "I can't breathe." He fought for his life the entire time that man kneeled on his neck with all *his* strength. Perry's bravery gave me the courage to go out and do something to help people recognize his humanity and to extend his voice. His voice was silenced, but I can be his voice now, by setting down the words in this book.

Another reason Black people ran out of patience is the hold that white supremacy has on our society. There are people walking around who like to say that once the Civil Rights Act and the Voting Rights Act were passed in the 1960s, that was the end of racism in America, that Black and white people were made equal by those laws and now had equal opportunities. That couldn't be further from the truth. American institutions are just as racist as they ever were; it's just that what used to be hung on a big banner outside the courthouse is now hidden inside the concrete.

No matter what white folks perceive as progress for Black people, our civic institutions—city councils, state legislatures, police forces, courts, schools—are run by white citizens for white citizens. At best, we're invisible; the white people who run things just don't see us. They ignore our neighborhoods or our own institutions. When they do see us, they see us as inferior, as less than, when they don't see us as a threat. A lot of attitudes toward the Black community and individual Black people haven't changed much since the days of slavery. There are aspects of our lives that never really changed because white people are desperate to hold power. They just found other ways over the years to set policies that would benefit themselves at the expense of Black people.

During the time of slavery, the owner of a plantation or the white overseer of the workers could and would punish the slaves for any type of minor fault. You could get beaten and whipped for not working hard enough, or having a conversation, or just having the wrong look on your face. If a white person killed a slave while beating or whipping him or her, there were no consequences for the person who caused the death. They were immune from prosecution. We have the same thing today. It's called qualified immunity.

Under qualified immunity, a police officer who grievously injures or even kills a suspect doesn't face prosecution, can't be hauled into court for hurting or even killing someone. Police officers today have the same protection that overseers on the plantation had in the 1800s. And you can't get rid of it because of the deep layers of systemic racism. It isn't that different from the days of slavery. Qualified immunity has been institutionalized for everyone in law enforcement, which is overwhelmingly white, because white people will not give up control over Black people. It's a get-out-of-jail-free card for white police and takes away any notion of accountability.

Another aspect of law enforcement that has roots in the time of slavery is racial profiling. Most schoolchildren learn about the Fugitive Slave Act, which was passed by the U.S. Congress in 1850, when a lot of slaves were escaping to freedom in the North. The law called for anyone who suspected a person of being a slave to turn in that person to police; if you protected a slave from being returned to the master, you faced prison and a stiff fine. Hundreds of free Black people were kidnapped and accused of being escaped slaves, and a lot of them *became* slaves because their cases came before commissioners at hearings where the accused person had no rights usually granted to defendants. And the commissioner was paid twice as much if he found the Black person to be a slave.

It isn't a big stretch to compare the fate of Black people under the Fugitive Slave Act to the way police officers racially profile Black people today. If a call goes out to the police that a suspect in a robbery is a "young Black man, medium height and build," police will stop or pull over every Black man under forty who isn't a mountain or a pebble. Racial profiling makes every Black person an object of suspicion for white people. It puts a target on all our backs. Because Perry was a Black man with a felony record and an allegedly fake twenty-dollar bill, he was Derek Chauvin's target.

That's one of the reasons we're out of patience. The system has never really changed; it just got rerouted into different forms. Okay, we aren't subject to the Fugitive Slave Act anymore, but police officers and sheriffs' deputies are still busting people for Living While Black. We don't get whipped in the fields today, but law enforcement officials can still get away with killing Black people. This is the twenty-first century. It's ridiculous that these things keep happening.

White supremacy is huge, and it isn't going away. White people just don't want people of color to be seen as equal to them. In order for white Americans to see the value in changing their attitudes toward us, they have to see us as human beings. We have to get past a way of thinking that sends a white person with a drug problem to rehab and a Black person with a drug problem to jail.

We got off to a bad start with that, because the first 250 years Black people lived in America, most of us weren't human beings at all—we were property to be bought and sold, used until we were used up. Then we were no longer slaves, but we were definitely second-class citizens, treated differently from white people. We were even used as lab animals, as in the notorious Tuskegee Syphilis Study. Black women considered "mentally deficient" were sterilized in much greater numbers than white women during the twentieth century, in some states into the 1970s.

We were never really seen as human beings, and in order to treat people with humanity, you have to see every person as a human being. Ironically, most Black people have always seen white people as human beings. In fact, the sad thing, when I was growing up, was that most of us in the Black community actually saw white people as being better than we were. That's what we were taught by our parents. They told us that to keep us safe, but it was also convenient for white supremacists because that's exactly how they wanted it.

It's a fact of white supremacy that you can be a dirt-poor, uneducated white person and look at a Black person and say, "Well, I'm better than he is, because I'm not Black." And the world supports that opinion because in a lot of places, even a dirt-poor, uneducated white person will be treated better than a Black person. Even a guy in the trashiest, dented-up pickup truck doesn't get pulled over if he's white. A white woman has to look like she's literally living on the streets before a clerk will follow her around in a store.

Many people think the developmentally disabled don't have racial prejudice because they don't know enough to treat Black and white people differently, but in many cases, they do know. When I was first out of college, more than thirty years ago, I worked at a group home for developmentally disabled adults in Iowa. I loved all my patients, but my favorite was a guy named Tim. He had Down syndrome; he wasn't high functioning, more like moderately disabled.

One day, he got mad at me because I wouldn't give him a second snack. I said, "You know how it is, the dietitian doesn't want you to have it because we got to look out for the diabetes." But Tim didn't want to hear that. He looked at me intensely, stuck out his chest, and started to pound it like he was King Kong. Then he started to stutter, "Nuh-nuh-nuh-nuh." I kept my cool and tried to get him to calm down, but he kept saying, "Nuh-nuh-nuh-nuh." Finally, he hit his chest and came out with the word he was trying to say: "You nigger!"

Tim had to have been taught that word, either at the group home, where he'd been living for at least fifteen years, or earlier. He could have thrown a tantrum or called me another name, like "stupid" or even "bitch." He knew I worked there, that I was smart, and I was there to help him. But he'd taken in the idea that I wasn't as good as he was because he was white and I was a nigger. I will never forget that as long as I live.

One time I was in a store, and I had just paid with a hundred-dollar bill. Before the clerk accepted the bill, she put it through a scanner to make sure it was legitimate. The next person in line, a white lady, was also paying with a hundred-dollar bill. I had a feeling that they weren't going to check her bill. And they didn't! The same clerk who put my bill through the scanner didn't check hers. That's not right! I learned you have to talk to the manager when something like that happens. You just can't let these things happen without saying something.

Some white people are nice and friendly to Black people during the day, but at night they see the very same Black folks they were friendly to during the day as a threat.

I will never forget the Hallmark experience and how fearfully the manager watched every move I did in the store. I was the same Angela I always was, but he had changed; he was uncomfortable being alone with a Black woman in his store at 9:30 p.m. He was fine with me when I shopped there in the daylight, when the store was full of people, but at 9:30 p.m., he saw a random Black woman who might make trouble. My dark skin had become a weapon. It always had been, but that became transparent when I was alone with him. He sold me the item I wanted, but I never went back to that store.

What gets me is that *I'm* the one who has to change my behavior. You can't get too comfortable with being yourself around people who aren't Black. It's like what I mentioned before, taking the stairs instead of the elevator because you don't want to make the white ladies in the elevator nervous. When I get exercised about something that happens, some slight or show of racial prejudice, I've got to regroup and say to myself, be careful; you can't do like they can because you're Black. I have to keep myself in check. It's exhausting.

We Black people talk about this kind of thing among ourselves. I share a lot of this stuff with my husband, my sisters, and my friends. When we talk about it, we give each other support and we say, "Yeah, this is what we've got to do. We have to deal with other people's attitudes. It's just what we have to do to survive in this world."

But things are different now because we don't give excuses for racist behavior anymore. Since Perry, my conversation is, "I'm tired; I don't want to deal with these attitudes anymore. I don't want to hear any excuses. My patience is done."

If that incident in the Hallmark store happened now, I would react differently. I'd tell the manager, "I can see you are uncomfortable with me. You're hesitating to sell me something because the color of my skin makes you afraid at this time of night. But I'm not here to hurt you. I just want to buy something I need before you close. I want you to know that I know where you're coming from." That's what I do now. I feel very good when I do that.

A lot of Black people are speaking up now who didn't used to speak up. They're going on social media and letting everybody know the inequalities and slights they face every day. They're calling out people who treat them badly instead of keeping quiet and changing their own behavior. If someone in a business like a store or a restaurant disrespects them, tries to make them feel less than, they complain, and they put the evidence, photographs and videos, on social media. They're speaking up to news media whenever some report makes Black people the villains of a story without any context or without all the facts. And they're speaking up loudly enough and in large enough numbers so that people have been fired from their jobs for racist behavior or speech. That means the business community is starting to listen.

I don't want Black kids today ever to keep their heads down and stay quiet the way we did. I'd tell them, "Your voice is your power now; you don't have to take what we did." We didn't know that our voices meant anything because we didn't think we were equal to white people. So when we were growing up, we let a few people like Martin Luther King Junior speak for us. When he was silenced, there weren't many Black people who could speak for us in a voice white people would listen to.

But no matter what, we kept alive, inside of us somewhere, the hope that things would get a little bit better. We took a lot of abuse from white supremacists, physical and psychological abuse, not because we liked it, not even because we didn't have a choice, but because we hoped things would get better for Black people someday. That's why we never gave up and continue to fight for equality today.

I'll tell any Black child that making things better takes a lot of struggle and a lot of courage. It isn't easy to tear down attitudes among whites *and* Blacks that were first shaped in this country by four hundred years of oppression. You have to be willing to lose your job, your freedom to walk around, even your life when you fight for what is right. You do what you have to do to make the future better for the next generation.

Maybe next year, things will be better. Maybe next year we will be able to move into that house. Maybe next year the bosses will bring our pay closer to white people's pay. Maybe next year the schools we send our kids to will have all the facilities that the schools have in white neighborhoods. Having hope for next year is why Black people have put up with a lot of this stuff. The problem always has been that Black people weren't in positions of enough power, and the people in the right positions didn't care about our hopes. That's why having a voice and raising it up is so important.

I will also tell children about my nephew Perry. I'll tell them that he wasn't Martin Luther King Junior. He was just a guy, and he had problems, but he was a human being with a heart and a soul. Perry asked for help—he asked to breathe, to live another day. I wish he were here to tell us how horrible it was to be under the knee of that police officer, how terrifying it was to have someone choke the life out of you when you're handcuffed and helpless. He hung in there until he couldn't any longer, but the world saw his struggle and the vicious way he was murdered.

It isn't important that Perry had drugs in his system. His dependency was a disease; if he'd been in a wheelchair or dragging an oxygen tank and the officers had done what they did, the outcry would have been even stronger, but Perry's disease, his challenges, counted against him. His disease gave the police what they thought was a good reason to abuse him, just the way police have justified abuse or even murder of people with psychological diseases like schizophrenia or developmental disorders like autism. They'd claim, "The suspect was acting strangely," or "The suspect was disruptive," without stopping to ask why. Perry was no different. He gave his life so that millions of people, Black and white and every other kind of person, would say, "Enough. We've seen enough of this, and we're going to do something about it."

Left: Great grandfather Hillary Thomas Stewart and great grandmother Larcenia Stewart (who George's mother was named after).

From left: William Stewart, Hillary Thomas Stewart (born January 3, 1897, George Perry Floyd's great grandfather), great aunts Brazilla and Ella, and uncle Lester Stewart. These are Hillary Thomas Stewart and Larcenia Stewart's children. They had twenty kids together—five are shown here.

*George Floyd's
great-grandmother,
Sophell Suggs Stewart.*

*George Floyd's grandmother
Laura Ann Jones Stewart
(Angela Harrelson's
mother).*

From left: George Perry Floyd, Sr. (Father), Cissy, Larcenia Floyd (Holding her son George Perry Floyd, Jr.), LaTonya Floyd, and Zsa Zsa Floyd (George Floyd's sisters)—1970s.

Aunt Angela Harrelson with her sister Cissy, Larcenia Floyd (George Floyd's mother) in North Carolina.

George Perry Floyd

Vikas Narula (left), George Floyd, and his best friend/roommate Alvin Manago take a ride on a sailboat.

Left: Aunt Mahalia Jones, Aunt Angela Harrelson, First Cousin Paris Stevens, and Aunt Laura Stevens, North Carolina. Artist Sidney Brodie presented his sixty-foot quilt project "The Elephant in the Room" on Tuesday, May 25th, 2021 at the "Rise & Remember" George Floyd 1st Year Anniversary Celebration. Sidney did a Quilt Ceremony in honor of George Floyd, which took place near the "Say Their Names" Cemetery at George Floyd Square.

Taken at the 1st Year Anniversary Celebration, "Rise & Remember." In the front row, the Floyd family sits with other families whose loved ones were killed by the police.

Photograph by nephew Shawn Jones, 2020

The Floyd family riding the bus along Houston Highway, watching crowds along the showing their support. It seems like never-ending miles long.

Photograph by nephew Shawn Jones, 2020

In Houston, the Floyd family was about to enter Houston Memorial Gardens where George Perry Floyd was going to be buried. We came to a sudden stop because of the crowds ahead. When the crowd saw us pull up, they graciously moved out of the way, yelling their support. Say his name, "George Floyd."

The Fountain of Praise Church in Houston hosted the funeral service.

Three of our amazing volunteers, Heather, Paul, and Tari, at Pillsbury House and Theatre. who all work with trained art conservators from Midwest Art Conservation Center to clean and archive all offerings laid to rest by people all over the world who shared their grief, pain, love, and support after the death of George Floyd. So far, they have archived over 3,000 pieces of artwork (paintings, drawings, signs, flowers, and letters) to soon place in a museum, the George Floyd Global Memorial.

Photograph by Rachel Austin, Chasing Joy Photography 2021

George Floyd's 1st Anniversary Celebration—May 25, 2021. From left: Laura Stevens, Mahalia Jones (Aunt), Carry Bandy Wright (Cousin), and Angela Harrelson (Aunt).

Photograph by Rachel Austin, Chasing Joy Photography 2021

At George Floyd's Square 1st Year Anniversary Celebration in 2021. Aunt Angela Harrelson, and First Cousin Paris Stevens.

CHAPTER 4

The Runaway Slave Mentality and the Police

I was working on the planning stages of the event that would mark the first anniversary of Perry's death when I heard the news about Daunte Wright. I hadn't even been sure whether we would have an event, but I felt the community needed something to look forward to. We needed to see people together, coming together with hope that we are rising together as a community. It was starting to be exciting to think about who would speak, who would sing, what else would be involved.

Then the phone rang.

A cousin said, "Did you hear the news? The police killed another unarmed Black man in Minnesota."

"Are you sure?" I asked.

"Yeah, I'm sure," she said. "Turn the news on."

I logged on to Facebook and saw a video of people marching and protesting, but I still didn't really believe it. Then I found a news clip with more details, and that made me start calling people who hold vigils at George Floyd Square because they hear everything. Finally, I got hold of someone who told me that several community leaders at the square had rushed to Brooklyn Center, where the latest killing had happened. That's when I knew it was true.

Until that moment, I had held some hope in my heart that things would get better, that Perry's murder might bring about some positive change in how police interacted with Black people. That light of hope grew bigger and bigger over the summer, fall, and winter, bigger and bigger, brighter and brighter—then: *bam*. Another Black man, Daunte Wright, was dead, not ten miles from where Perry had been killed.

It really set me back. It took me a minute to decompress my feelings and reflect on this new story. I didn't want to see anybody; I didn't even want to go to court. I was trying to be strong enough to get through each day, grieve for Perry, follow the trial, and this new killing, just the kind of thing we were struggling against, was like a punch to the stomach. My heart went out to Daunte's family, and I wanted to be with them, but I just didn't have the strength. I didn't have the energy to get in my car and drive to Brooklyn Center.

After some reflection, I brought up the image of Perry summoning his last fumes of energy to say, "I can't breathe." I was able to take those last words and channel them through my inner need to be a voice for my people. I decided to use the same energy Perry had shown by standing in solidarity with the Wright family. I went to Daunte's funeral and spent some time with his mother. It was difficult for me to do, but it was the right thing to do.

Daunte Wright's death made me realize more than ever that we had to get the verdict right in Perry's killing, to get a guilty verdict. America has to get it right.

What happened to Perry is what happens all too often when a Black person is arrested for a crime, compared with what happens when a white person is arrested. Police often will use over-whelming force against Blacks because they see us as threatening and dangerous. A white person under arrest? The officer treats the white person with much less aggression, almost as if he's a family member and the cop regrets having to take him in.

It's like when Dylann Roof was arrested for killing nine Black people studying the Bible in South Carolina. While they were taking him to the police station, Roof said he was thirsty, and the police got him some water. Then they bought him something at Burger King. That would never happen with a Black suspect.

It's not just Perry, of course. Some police officers think the Fugitive Slave Act, which I mentioned in the previous chapter, is still in force and that their job is to return Blacks to their rightful owners. In their minds, the "rightful owners" are the courts and the prisons, and that's where they think Black people belong.

The practice of capturing people bound to service and returning them to where they ran away from goes back further than the establishment of the United States. Colonial laws concerning the return of fugitives were in place from the early 1700s, and the idea that servants belonged with their masters was enshrined in our Constitution from 1789:

> *No person held to service or labor in one state, under the laws thereof, escaping into another, shall, in consequence of any law or regulation therein, be discharged from such service or labor, but shall be delivered up on claim of the party to whom such service or labor may be due.* (U.S. Constitution, Article IV, Section 3)

This instruction in the Constitution, that people bound to service had to be returned to their servitude, was expanded in the Fugitive Slave Act of 1793. The federal law stated that someone "to whom such labor or service may be due" could assign an agent or attorney to capture a fugitive and take him or her before a judge or magistrate. The agent of the "owner" was supposed to prove that the person had indeed run away, and if the official determined that the fugitive owed service to another person, it was his duty to let the agent take the fugitive back. (The word "slave" never appears in the law because the U.S. didn't want to acknowledge that it allowed slavery.) Also, anyone who was caught helping a fugitive hide or escape was fined $500 (more than $14,000 in today's money).

Many states north of the Mason-Dixon Line and the Ohio River resisted sending back fugitive slaves and passed laws stating that any Black person within their borders was free, no matter where he or she came from, and couldn't be removed to go back into servitude. In 1842, the Supreme Court ruled that states could forbid their officials from cooperating in the return of fugitive slaves. But it also established that the federal government, not the states, had the ultimate responsibility for the legal status of slaves. In its decision, the court also ignored the problem of free Blacks being kidnapped and sold into slavery. It implied, without saying directly, that Black people had fewer legal protections than whites.

By the 1840s, the slave states of the South had so much power in Congress that they were able to pass the Fugitive Slave Act of 1850. Under that law, all government officials, including those in free states, were required to arrest people suspected of being runaway slaves or risk a $1,000 fine (equal to about $34,000 today), and any private citizen who helped a runaway slave faced the same fine and six months in jail. The suspected slave had no rights in court and couldn't even testify. Commissioners who heard these cases were paid ten dollars if they declared the suspect was indeed a fugitive and five dollars if they thought the proof was insufficient. Officers who arrested fugitive slaves were given bonuses and promotions.

Patrols of men looking for runaway slaves had existed since the early 1700s, and with the passage of the Fugitive Slave Act of 1850, the slave-catching business boomed. Bounty hunters roamed across the United States, which by then covered most of the land it has today, picking up suspected fugitives. A slave patrol could enter anyone's home—by force, if necessary—looking for escaped slaves. Any Black person, free or not, could be arrested and brought before a commissioner as a suspected fugitive, and many free Blacks were enslaved in the process.

The use of patrols to round up runaway slaves was a model—maybe not the only model, but definitely a model—for the establishment of official police forces in America.

This was especially true in the South, but even big-city police forces in the North during the nineteenth century were all male, almost all white, and formed to respond to disorder more than to crime. They were expected to control groups considered part of a "dangerous underclass," including Black people, poor people, and immigrants. There weren't many standards for hiring and training police officers until the early twentieth century. Many police officers routinely used violence against the groups they targeted without any consequences, and that's still true today.

All these factors—the instruction to keep order, lack of adequate training, not nearly enough police officers of color, a culture of violence, and the police forces' roots in slave patrols—are an influence on policing to this day. These factors haven't changed much in the past four hundred years, and they've been reinforced by laws and court rulings that give police more and more power and allow judges to convict and sentence Black people more harshly than whites. Many people, and not just Black people, call for police "reform," but many others see the oppression of

Black people as something so embedded in police forces' history and culture that it can't be "reformed" away.

That's why I think there's such a close resemblance between the slave patrols of the 1850s and police officers' constant profiling of Black people as potential suspects. They keep looking at us as stereotypes. If, when you see a Black person, the first things you think are "aggressive," "violent," "dangerous," "be extra careful," "doesn't belong here," that's going to be in your mind no matter how much you train, and it's going to lead you to a bad decision. Your mind might be saying, "Find out what the situation is," but your instincts say, "He is dangerous. Subdue him." And because you pull out a gun instead of a TASER to subdue him, the way it happened with Daunte Wright, you shoot him dead.

It's been like this since the beginning of the Jim Crow era. When police officers see these brown and Black people, they may not see them as actual slaves, but they see them as not their equals. They see them as second-class citizens, maybe not even as human beings. It's pretty much automatic.

At best, in this "us" versus "them" mentality: The Black suspect is an enemy soldier, one of "them" that we need to stop. He's someone dangerous, violent—someone the officer needs to handcuff immediately. This is the mindset in racial profiling that police officers are trained to have. They go into every situation with their minds already made up. They're out there to feed the criminal justice system as present-day slave catchers.

Too many police officers lose their grip on reality when they deal with Black people: they have tunnel vision and see all of us as potential criminals. Now, there are some good police officers out there. That's a fact. But even good officers don't help with the problem of oppressive policing because they don't stand up to their racist colleagues. If you go along with what's been going on and you're not doing anything about it, you're not solving the problem; you're part of it. "Go along, get along" is a common refrain in police precincts, and police officers generally keep quiet about fellow officers' misdeeds. They know that reporting police misdeeds opens them to a world of hurt. This is especially true for rookies, who are under huge pressure to conform to a precinct's practices. The two rookie officers who were present when Perry was killed may have been appalled by Derek Chauvin's actions, but they didn't move a muscle to help Perry.

I think Kim Potter, the officer who shot Daunte Wright, wanted to reach for her TASER instead of her gun, and I think she was genuinely horrified that she had shot him. But that doesn't excuse her for the shooting. She had twenty-six years on the force. She knew all the guidelines for using force. She'd been a training officer, for heaven's sake. She was immersed in the politics of policing. It doesn't matter that Potter meant to pull out her TASER instead of her gun.

Even though the shooter won't admit profiling and stereo-typing Black men, people will probably empathize with her. They'll say, "Well, she made a mistake. Anybody can make a mistake." But it wasn't really a mistake—it was a bad decision. When you make a mistake, you have no intention of doing something wrong. But Officer Potter meant to subdue Daunte Wright using a weapon. I think her subconscious, the part of her mind that believed any young Black man was a threat, overrode her weapons training and said, "Grab your gun."

All the blame cannot be placed on her regarding her fatal decision. It's the corrupt system. The consequences of the ugly systemic racism that was put in place against brown and Black people worked against their own.

Often police officers grew up in small towns and as adults live in those small towns and in white suburbs, so they didn't meet people from diverse backgrounds as kids and don't mix with them now. That's a problem because if they grew up among white people and live among them now, they really don't see people of color as neighbors or possible friends. The Black people they see on the job are The Other, and to some of them, they're barely people at all.

People are always calling for police reform. but it's very difficult to reform a mind that has been the same way for twenty years or more. It isn't impossible because God can change anybody's heart, but you have to be open to the change. That's why police have to be trained from their first day at the academy to see every single person they come in contact with as a human being and to bring down the temperature of every encounter. To de-escalate. I don't know how many veteran officers police departments are going to be able to retrain that way. They have to start somewhere, though.

To my mind, there's a difference between a bad decision and a mistake. A mistake is an action taken without intent to cause harm. You make a bad decision when you know there will be negative consequences of your actions, but you do it anyway. Police, hospital workers, and all frontline responders are trained about the carotid artery. If it's cut off for more than five to ten seconds, there can be brain damage or death. The police officer who killed Perry had had that training. He knew exactly what happens when you squeeze shut the carotid artery, and he decided to kneel on Perry's neck for nine minutes anyway. That was a bad decision. People will make mistakes because they are human, and they shouldn't necessarily be punished for their mistakes. But bad decisions should be punished, because if there are no consequences for bad decisions, nothing will ever change.

Racial profiling needs to just go away. Most people in prison are Black or brown, but the United States is still a majority of white people. We Black people can't be the only ones who are shoplifting. We can't be the only ones boosting cars, and we for sure aren't the only ones dealing drugs.

Black kids plead guilty to crimes they didn't commit because they are scared; the police tell them they'll do a lot more time if they're found guilty by a jury. They interrogate Black people for hours, telling them the only way they can do themselves any good is if they confess, leaning on them until they do confess for something they didn't do. That's what happened to those boys in New York thirty years ago, the Central Park Five. They were all Black teenagers who went to prison for rape because the interrogators wouldn't leave them alone until they confessed. And you still have bad police who plant drugs or a weapon on somebody just to get a conviction and to make themselves look good.

The inequity happens time after time after time. If a white kid is caught with drugs, he'll probably go into treatment while the Black kid goes to jail. If someone acts strange because he has a mental illness, or maybe he's autistic, the police will take him to the emergency room if he's white, but if he's Black, again, he's going to jail—if he doesn't get shot. Jail isn't a treatment center or a hospital. For one thing, the person who is taken for treatment doesn't come out with a criminal record.

It just breaks my heart. Some of these kids who get into trouble are fourteen or fifteen years old. They may make mistakes, they get into stuff, but what they don't have is anyone guiding them. A lot of Black boys don't have positive male role models in their lives. Imagine if instead of arresting a Black kid, a police officer said, "Look, I don't want you to lose your freedom. This is what you need to do to stay out of trouble." If you put that boy on the right path, it can make a huge difference in his life because once he's in the criminal justice system, he's just on a path to more crime and more punishment.

A lot of brown and Black men are afraid. They honestly think they are going to be killed. They think if they get out of the car, they are going to be killed. "Even if you raise your hands up in the air, with nothing in them," they think, "you are going to be killed. You put your hands down, you are going to be killed. You say you can't read, you are going to be killed. If you cooperate, you are going to be killed. If you don't cooperate, you are going to be killed." They don't know what to do. No matter what they do, someone gets killed. I understand why they're afraid to cooperate because what difference does it make? They're going to get shot.

Perry did what he was supposed to do. He walked with those police officers, explained that he was claustrophobic and didn't want to be in the police car, lay down on the ground, and let them cuff him. He cried, begged them to tell him why he was being arrested, asked them to tell his daughter he loved her, told them he couldn't breathe. And they mocked him; they said, "You're talking; you must be able to breathe." Then they killed him. And when everybody watching asked, "Why did you do that?" they said Perry was resisting arrest, which he never did. Not for one second.

Another example of racial profiling and inequality is the extent of the check officers do during traffic stops after you've given them your license and registration. Those checks can be much more extensive on people of color than on white people. If a white person is pulled over for a minor violation, the officer will probably do a quick check to see if the person has unpaid tickets and whether the license is valid. Then the officer returns to the car, writes the ticket, and sends the driver on his or her way. The whole thing takes two or three minutes. That's what happened one day when I was riding with a white friend.

But a Black driver is likely to sit for a longer time because the officer is checking multiple databases: for outstanding warrants, for previous misdemeanors and felonies, for ownership of a weapon, plus the usual violations and parking tickets. If I get stopped, I know I'm going to be sitting there for a while.

I've had one bad experience with a police officer during a traffic stop, when I was so sick that I was driving myself to the hospital. I have a thyroid condition, and at that time, it was unregulated. My heart was beating really fast, and the medication I was on was making me throw up. I didn't have my seatbelt on, and my car was like wavering in the lane a little bit because I felt so awful.

A police officer pulled me over and said he was stopping me for not wearing a seatbelt. I told him, "Sure, I understand," and I said I was really sick and trying to get to the hospital, which was just six or seven blocks away. I waited while he ran his check, and when he came back, he gave me a ticket for the seatbelt violation and told me I needed to leave right away. But I needed a few minutes to collect myself. I was still throwing up, getting worse, wondering if I could even make it to the hospital.

Then the officer came up to the car again and asked, "What are you doing still here?"

I said, "Sir, I was throwing up and I was trying to get myself together so I can get to the hospital."

"You need to leave," he said. "You need to leave right now."

"Can you help me?" I asked. "Can you call 911? Because I'm just getting worse. I don't know if I can drive the rest of the way."

"You need to leave right now, or you are going to get another ticket," the officer said. "Leave now." I said, "Yes, sir," and drove the rest of the way to the hospital.

All that police officer cared about was giving me that ticket. He didn't care about me being sick. He was 911. If he had seen me as an equal, as a human being, he would have called an ambulance or followed me to the hospital. But he didn't care. All he cared about was that I didn't do exactly what he had told me to do.

Right now, I don't think any Black person trusts the police. The officers are too trigger-happy around Black people. A Black person leaves a place thinking, "I just hope I get home alive." I see white people doing things that I would never do because people would come after me. Life is too short to stand there and think, "Gee, I wish I could get away with that." I just say to myself, "I'm a Black person and I know I have to be more careful."

The people of color whom officers pull over or confront on the street, or in their own houses, aren't mass murderers. They didn't blow up a building; they aren't terrorists. Almost every time, they're people who never hurt anybody and just want to get home. For them to be forced onto the ground, to be pepper sprayed, to be handcuffed, let alone killed, is just insane. Most of my relatives are probably scared of the police now, from my sister, who is almost eighty years old, down to my youngest grandnieces and grandnephews. And now I'm afraid of the police too. I was always nervous around the police, but when Perry was killed, the anxiety got worse and I became afraid. I'm scared that if a police officer stops me, especially at night, I won't know whether I'm going to live or die.

Derek Chauvin was written up for using excessive force again and again, and nobody did anything about it. The police department wasted a lot of time finding excuses for his misconduct. His superiors could have spent that time retraining Chauvin and all his fellow officers. They could have said, "You know what? This has to stop. We're not going to allow our police officers to use excessive force anymore. We're going to teach you how to bring down the temperature of a situation so that nobody, including you, gets hurt, and once you've learned that, we're going to hold you accountable if you cross the line."

When police are protected by qualified immunity, their wrong-doing never sees the light of day, let alone gets punished. I'm a registered nurse. If I make a mistake that harms a patient, I'm definitely held accountable. I don't have qualified immunity. Most professionals who serve the public don't have qualified immunity, and those who do aren't as protected by it as police officers are. A doctor who harms a patient gets sued. A teacher who hits a kid is yanked out of the classroom that day. Why should a police officer almost always get a pass?

Police departments need to clean house of officers who can only think "us versus them," and to hire leaders and officers with fresh minds to end racial profiling once and for all. They need to train police to see everyone they come in contact with as a fellow human being, not a wild animal or an enemy soldier. If you can't see people who don't look like you as human beings, then you shouldn't be a police officer. No one, of any color, who gets pulled over for a minor traffic violation should end up dead at the hands of a trigger-happy police officer.

They need to bring in young people who are less engaged in stereotyping and more committed to providing equal protection. I don't believe in what people call "reform." It's too late for reform.

How do you re-educate somebody who has been policing the same way for twenty-plus years? We have to start over and get it right.

My sister, who's almost eighty years old, asked me, "Angela, why do they hate us so much?" I know not all white people hate us, and I told her they don't all hate us, but that's how she feels.

There is a glimmer of hope: I think more white people are starting to understand systemic racism within the police department since Perry died. One day that summer, a lady came up to me in a restaurant and said, "I just want to say I'm so sorry how my people are mistreating you all. It is not right." She said she finally saw the difference between how Black people and white people are regarded and treated. It made me feel good that she would walk up to me and say that.

I've been helping with the memorial to Perry in Minneapolis. It's grown to include tributes to a lot of Black people who were killed by the police, especially young people. One day I was there with my little niece, who is seven, and as we looked at the home-made tombstones, she spotted one that was for a seven-year-old girl. She couldn't believe the police had killed someone her own age. "Aunt Angela, are they going to kill me too?" she asked me.

"No," I said. "They are not going to kill you. You're safe." But how do you convince a little girl that police who shot a child her age won't shoot her too? And when I tell her she's safe, how do I know that's even true? It just wrenches my heart that a seven-year-old has to ask that question.

But right after that, a white lady came over to us. She had seen my niece and heard our conversation. She asked my niece's name and told us her name, and I told her how we were related to Perry. Then she said to my niece, "I just want you to know, you have a lot to be proud of. Your cousin is a hero in my mind. He changed the world for the better, and things *are* changing for the better. You have that to look forward to, and it is going to be better." And we smiled. I hear those comments every day. But still...when I think about the differences between how whites live and how Blacks live, I tell myself, "Mm, it must be good to be white." I'll explain why in the next chapter.

CHAPTER 5

It Must Be Good to Be White

You would think that after all this time and all that's been said and written about racism, white people would understand systemic racism and want to do something about it. Unfortunately, that's just not true.

It's this simple: most white people, rich or poor, grow up feeling that they're better than people whose skin is darker, whose facial features are different. That feeling spreads into every aspect of life: employment, housing, schools, health care, government. Now Black people finally have said they've had enough; they want the same opportunities for a good education, the same access to livable housing and jobs that pay decently, a real voice in government. That has made millions of white people angry. They don't want us on their level because that takes away some of the privilege they've had just for being white.

The system treats Black and white people differently from the emergency room to the courtroom. Fear of Black people is rampant, and white people are quick to criminalize those of whom they're afraid. I worked with substance abusers; I saw that when a Black or brown person comes to a chemical dependency unit like mine, he can be labeled as dangerous immediately if he's wearing dreadlocks or has the hood of his sweatshirt pulled up. If he's yelling, he has to be subdued, and his dependency is seen as a failing on his part.

A white person, even if he's dressed the same way, doesn't inspire that kind of fear. His dependency is seen as a disease, and his yelling a form of self-expression. When my unit is handling a patient they categorize as dangerous and disruptive, I often step in and say, "What are we doing here? Let's give this person a chance. Let's see what this person is about before we make a decision that they're dangerous."

Even small things can make a difference in perception. For example, most hospitals don't have hair care products for Blacks. A lot of Black people can't use the same kind of combs that white people use, so they'll use a pick. But if a Black person comes into a hospital with a pick, sometimes the hospital staff treats it as a weapon and takes it away. Then they write on the chart that the person looks "disheveled"! *Of course* he looks disheveled—he doesn't have his pick, so he can't make his hair neat. At that point, the Black person in the hospital feels bad for two reasons: he's being judged unfairly, and his self-esteem suffers because he's a mess.

White people have no idea how fortunate they are that they aren't viewed as potential criminals every day of their lives. Racism is so baked into everything that affects our lives, people don't even notice it unless they're the ones being hurt. "Systemic" isn't just a word that you see in the news or in protests. It means racism is part of the system. This is how we are made to live. It's not just criminal justice issues. It's everyday living.

People get really nervous when they're around folks of a different group. I attend CPR classes every two years. In the early years of my nursing career in the '90s, when I'd sit down, I'd watch many of my white coworkers sit anywhere except the area in which I was sitting. Most would only sit near me if the place was crowded, and they didn't have a choice. That's an example of racist behavior: without speaking, people were saying, "I'm better than she is, and I don't want to sit by her."

Once I complained to the CPR instructor that there were no Black CPR dolls. Why should that be, I asked her, when people of all races need CPR? It sent a very wrong message. The white lady teaching the class was so surprised by my comment; I don't think the color of the dolls ever crossed her mind until I brought it up. Trust me, if white people went into a CPR class and all the practice dolls were Black, they'd notice. That was about twenty-five years ago, though. I'm happy to say that today, when I take a refresher in CPR, there are Black dolls to practice on.

Another example: When I was in military training, I was going to noncommissioned officer school to become a sergeant. There weren't many Blacks in the program, so I just tried to get along with everybody. I became friendly with a white girl who was very nice to me—when we were in class or by ourselves. But when she was in a group with other white people, she would ignore me. She didn't want them to know that she was hanging out with me. Don't think I didn't know it.

When I was a child, there was a white sharecropper's wife who always used to stop by our house. She'd idle the truck and talk to my mom, and she was always laughing and talking. She and my mom would talk and laugh together like old friends. But out in public, I would notice that this woman never introduced my mom to any of her white friends.

A few years later, her daughter went off to college and was matched with a Black roommate. Her mother questioned her daughter about sharing a room with a Black roommate. To her daughter's credit, she couldn't understand why her mother was disturbed by it. She reminded her mother about how she and my mom would hang around and talk and laugh together. And her mother didn't have a good answer; all she said was, "Well, sharing a room with that kind of girl, that isn't what we do."

That must have been a shock to the daughter because the message she received seeing her mother and mine laughing together was that it was fine for white and Black people to hang out together. No wonder she was surprised that her mother objected to a Black roommate. Fortunately, the earlier lesson stuck with the daughter to this day; she's a beautiful person who thinks nothing of being around Black people. What that young woman didn't know was that my mother knew she had an inferior status to her white friend and was fine with that. She considered it a privilege to laugh with someone who didn't look like her.

This happened a long time ago, but the racism is still with us. It's just hidden better. You never know how people really feel about you. Today, that mom wouldn't mention the roommate being Black; she'd say it would be better if her daughter had a roommate with the same major or somebody she had more in common with. Racists can hide what they believe about people of color for only so long. If you spend enough time with them, they will reveal themselves.

I also have my doubts about some of the people who are proclaiming themselves supporters of Black Lives Matter and other efforts toward equality. I think some of them just want to feel good about themselves, or they want to cover up their fear of Black people. It's sad because eventually they will be exposed too.

It's astonishing to Black people that white people don't recognize the systemic racism in everyday life because of their white privilege. A lot of white people deny that white privilege exists because they don't feel privileged. They think privilege is the same as having money, so if they aren't rich, they feel that being white doesn't bring them any privilege. Or if they do feel privileged, that privilege is something they earned, that they worked hard for.

But white privilege isn't about money. It's about what *doesn't* happen to you when you're white. If you have the privilege of white skin, you don't get second-guessed the way Black people do. In a hospital, you don't get mistaken for an orderly when you're a doctor. You don't get followed by salespeople in stores. You don't get pulled over for a broken taillight and find yourself cuffed and thrown facedown on the ground because you asked why the officer stopped you.

White people don't have to go to the police station when they move into a new neighborhood and explain, "I am a decent human being. I have a job. I just bought a house. Here are photos of our children. We are moving into the neighborhood. We belong here. We don't commit crimes. If you see my kids, please know that they belong here."

Systemic racism leaves a canyon between the way police officers treat Black people and the way they treat whites. Let's say a white teenager is caught drunk driving. Until not too long ago, the officers would just drive him home and tell him to take it easy on the drinking, maybe get some treatment. The same pair of officers would take a Black teenager caught drunk driving straight to jail, cutting him off from school, family, and work. The white boy escapes any punishment except what his parents might give him. The Black kid, however, gets a record, which will be a burden for him when he's looking for work. If that isn't systemic racism, I don't know what is.

I once was shopping with a white friend, and she saw some trim in a store window that looked like it would go with some fabric she had just bought in another store. She found the trim and said, "I'm just going to take this out to my car and see if it goes with the fabric I bought."

She started toward the front entrance with the trim. "Don't you have to pay for it first?" I asked.

"No, I'm coming right back with it," she said.

I watched her walk out, hold up the pack of trim to the fabric, and come back into the store. If I tried something like that, I'd be charged with shoplifting before I opened the car door.

But she just strolled out there like she didn't have a worry in the world and came back on in. The gal behind the cashier saw her leave the store and didn't say anything. I couldn't help it: I said, "Lord, it must be nice; it must be good to be white."

Another time I ran into a white gentleman I know, and he said to me, "Angela, you know, I'm getting really tired of these arguments over race. I'm not racist, I've never been racist, I don't have a racist bone in my body; but I'm tired of all the news being about police killing Black people. When is this going to end?"

"Uh-oh," I thought, but I said calmly, "When white privilege ends, the protests and the news reports will end."

"What are you talking about?" the man said. "I've never had white privilege in my life. I've earned everything I have, I got all my education on my own, I worked hard all my life."

I looked at him, still staying calm. "If you think white privilege is about how hard you worked, then you need to be informed because you're missing the point. White privilege has to do with an inherent membership that you got because you are white."

He looked at me skeptically.

"You may not have grown up rich, but you did grow up white," I said. "People didn't assume things about you that they did about us as Black. A lot of the time, the things we've wanted to accomplish in life have been out of our reach. We had to know our place and sit back. We came from a heritage where, at one time, it was illegal to teach Black people how to read and write. Then it was legal, but Black children went to segregated schools where the buildings were crumbling and the books were old and raggedy. Even today, in one city after another, schools where mostly white children go are nicer than schools that have mostly Black and brown children.

"You went to school with other white kids. When you applied to college, no one thought of you as a poor candidate for admission because you were white. Probably no one has ever turned you down for a job just because you're white. Having white skin gave you privileges that most people of color don't have. None of us are saying it's your fault. No one is trying to take away your college degrees, your work history, whatever success you've had."

He was listening.

"Your ancestors may not have been slaveowners, but your race benefited from slavery because you were recognized as human beings, not property," I said. "We just want the same opportunities and privileges you had because you were born white. We don't have them yet, so we're still fighting for them. I get that you are tired of seeing people marching in the streets, yelling, 'Black Lives Matter,' and chanting, 'No justice, no peace.' So imagine how tired Black people must be after fighting oppression in this country for four hundred years. Imagine how tired I am from struggling with racial prejudice for the fifty-nine years of my life, from watching my nephew die in a modern-day lynching. I'm exhausted from trying to tell people that I'm just as equal as you are, that I want to be treated fairly. My nephew should have been treated fairly. I have to fight for him, and Black people as a group must continue this fight for all people who were killed senselessly by the police."

Sometimes you get so tired that you question yourself. You ask yourself if you are doing the right thing, if it's enough—or too much. It can be very draining, but if you give in to the exhaustion and don't continue to raise your voice, then you fall into the trap that the white supremacists built for you. They want us to get tired. They want us to fall back, not push, shut up, and play the hand we were dealt. They like to remind us that at least we aren't slaves anymore.

Not everybody is that contemptuous, of course. But there are a lot of white Americans who think we're complaining too much because, as far as they're concerned, this problem got solved more than fifty years ago. Kids get taught in school about the Civil Rights Act and the Voting Rights Act and the Fair Housing Act, and they think the federal government got rid of racism in the 1960s. They learn about affirmative action and think Black folks have it made. They don't understand that affirmative action is about opening up opportunities, not taking anything away from white people. They hear about all these new state laws about voting restrictions and think of the restrictions as possible inconveniences; they don't see how they're meant to suppress voter turnout among people of color.

At the end of the day, white people still hold power and control over Black people in this country, and they do not want to give it up. One day, my older sister Laura parked her car on the street in Iowa, and a white guy who had been drinking drove into her car. Before the police arrived, the white man said to my sister, "You can call the police if you want, but they are not going to believe you because you're Black and I'm white. They will believe me over you." Even a drunk white person knows he can get away with behavior that a Black person can't. They know the white side is the better side.

My sister was scared to death. She had no idea what would happen to her as a Black woman alone facing down a white man—two white men, because the officer who responded would probably be white. Luckily for Laura, the officer (who was white) was a man of integrity. He told the drunk white guy, "I saw the whole thing, and it was your fault, not hers." My sister was happy and pleased; she never expected the officer to take her side. The point is that she was terrified because she expected to be a victim of white privilege. Neither she nor the white guy thought that would be the one time his privilege was revoked.

It isn't always a matter of life and death. I once went to some big function in a packed ballroom, and I couldn't find my husband. I went up to somebody wearing a headset, somebody who looked like staff, and I said, "Can you page my husband?"

"I don't know where you can do that," she replied, and she pointed to a security officer in the hall, a white man wearing a sharp suit and dark glasses. He was very nice and took me toward the front of the building.

"See that woman behind the desk?" the security man said. "She can help you." And then he disappeared; he didn't stay with me. I said to myself, 'I wish he hadn't left, because I don't know if that white lady is going to believe me.'"

I went over to the woman and said, "Miss, my name is Angela, and I need to page my husband because I can't find him. I lost him in that big ballroom upstairs, and he should know where I am."

She said, "I can't really help you. This phone is for emergency calls only, and we don't use it to page people for personal reasons."

"But the security man said I should talk to you."

"Well, where is he?"

"He showed me where you were, then I guess he went back to the hall outside the ballroom, where he's supposed to be."

"So he isn't here," the woman at the desk said.

"I'm not making this up," I said. "A security officer said I should come to you and tell you that I need to page my husband and you would help me."

"I don't see any security officer," she said.

My face got hot. I knew what was going on. I was the complaining Black lady who was breaking up her nice, quiet evening shift. I went back up to the ballroom and found the security officer who helped me before.

"Sir," I said, "the lady at the front desk doesn't believe me. She doesn't believe you sent me to her for help. Are you able to come with me for a minute?"

"Sure," he said, and he went back to the front of the building with me. We found the woman, and the security man told her that he had sent me to her desk because he didn't know how to page anyone and he figured she would.

"Oh, okay," the woman said. "I guess I can help her."

"Thank you so much, sir," I said to the security man. He smiled and went back upstairs. "See, you didn't believe me until that man came down here with me. And it's because I'm Black, right?"

"No, not at all," she said and rolled her eyes. "You just didn't tell me what you really wanted." Then she spun out a few more untruths, but I knew. I knew she wouldn't take my word without backup from the white security guard.

White people don't have to do so many things I feel I have to do. If I see a police vehicle when I'm driving, I drive away from it, even if that takes me out of my way. At the grocery store, I get my shopping done fast because if you linger, some white staff member will start to watch you. Wherever I spend money, I make sure I get a receipt so no one can tell me I stole something. These are things that white people don't have to think about because they are not Black.

Sometimes I say to myself, "White folks sure got it made, just walking in stores and not having to be worried about anything except the price of what they want to buy. It certainly would be nice one day to be treated like any white person, to be judged only for how I behave in an everyday way. Not labeled. Not followed. Not profiled. Not suspected."

White Americans don't understand how lucky they are that other white folks look at them and don't assume immediately that they're aggressive or lazy or violent or dumb. They've always thought of themselves—and always have been made to look—like the better race. No white person can understand what systemic racism is when the system always treats him as a member of the better race.

Black people are often in situations where they are one or two people in a sea of white people. That's why there are so many all-Black churches and social groups, why it's so important for us to have a culture we can relate to on our own. It's more comfortable.

Let's say there's a big crowd, and I'm the only Black person in the crowd. Everybody's just walking along, and out of nowhere, someone yells the n-word. Who do you think they're going to look at? I guarantee, if someone yells the n-word, everybody is going to look at me because the n-word means only one thing, and that's a Black person. Even the most enlightened, sophisticated white person who has known me for fifteen years is going to look at me and not anyone else. After that, she might look around to see who yelled the n-word, she might apologize to me for a white person's rudeness, she might even scold the person who said it, but the first thing she's going to do is look for the Black person. That's how powerful the n-word is.

Some white people like to point out that many Black people use the n-word among themselves, but that's completely different. Some Black folks have sort of reclaimed the n-word and use it to show solidarity with each other. It's a little like some women will call each other the b-word as if they're saying "sister" or "girlfriend." But if a man flings the b-word at a woman, he's just being insulting. It's the same thing with the n-word. Black people can use it with each other, but it's off-limits to other folks.

It's a controversy in the Black community. I don't use it because for me, it's like repeating the hatred that has been directed at us for so long. The word puts that hatred inside me. I don't want it to be there, and I don't want to take a chance of insulting someone who doesn't want to hear it. But there are people in my family who use it, and I don't scold them when they do. It's why Black people who do use that word spell and pronounce it as if it has an "a" at the end, instead of "er."

Can a white person step into an all-Black church and feel comfortable? Can he attend an all-Black meeting of Alcoholics Anonymous and share without being self-conscious? If someone is injured downtown and taken to an emergency room where most everybody is a person of color, will he be confident that he's getting good care? Most of them never find out because white people rarely have to put themselves in situations where they're the tiny minority. White Christians go to predominantly white churches and look for AA meetings where most people look like them. If he has the insurance, the white guy who got hurt downtown probably will ask not to be taken to the inner-city hospital. But a lot of Black people are in situations like that all the time: in class, in Scout troops, at work, in the military.

Once I was sitting in a car parked on the street with one of my white friends, and two or three young Black guys ran by the car.

She jumped, startled, and locked the door where she was sitting. Then she looked at me, and she said, "Oh, I'm sorry, Angela, I didn't mean to do that."

"Yes, but you did it," I said. "You got nervous, even though you were sitting in the car with your Black friend and those boys weren't doing anything but running on the sidewalk. I knew they didn't mean any harm. But, right away, you saw them as a threat."

Not only that, but the boys probably heard the door lock. When somebody uses the term "microaggression," that's exactly the kind of little thing he means. It still hurts.

This was a woman whom I considered a good friend. We'd gone out to dinner together and eaten at each other's homes. We'd done business together. I'd known her for more than ten years. And still, it was in her to treat my people differently, and even me. She said she was embarrassed. "You're embarrassed because you got caught doing something racist," I said.

You miss out on the beauty of life when you let your fears keep you from learning about different cultures and embracing them. Maybe there is some risk involved, but the risk is definitely worth it when you start to feel comfortable around people who are different from you, and you aren't scared of them anymore. When you fear Black people, you turn our skin color into a weapon. Again, I ask: How can the color of someone's skin be a weapon?

It's also frustrating to hear white people talk about racism as a problem of the past, as if all the civil rights legislation solved everything. As I mentioned before, that plays a big role in systemic racism. They ignore the programs set up to help Black people that don't exist anymore, and the laws and court decisions that actually have taken away some of the rights Black people fought for in the 1960s and have kept white people in control. And if you remind them of what federal, state, and local governments have done that harms the Black community, they'll say, "I'm not part of the government. I have nothing to do with that." It's the flip side of people saying, "You can't blame me for slavery and Jim Crow laws because I wasn't born yet." Just as white people benefited from slavery and Jim Crow, they benefit today from government policies that harm Blacks.

Many white people only become concerned about society's problems when they are affected directly. Look at the use of addictive drugs. When crack cocaine was destroying Black families and neighborhoods, white people were mostly oblivious to the damage it was doing and how many Black people were being put in jail because of it. But when millions of white people became addicted to opiates, all they could talk about was the need for detox and rehab programs.

One of the strangest things about racial hatred is the idea white people have that any gains we make come at their expense. They see the world as a pie that isn't getting any bigger, so if Black people get more, white people must get less. Many of them are scared to death that Black people might actually get ahead of white people somehow. The most extreme white people oppose policies that benefit Blacks *even if those policies benefit them too.*

This is sad and foolish on two levels. First of all, white privilege was so unchallenged for so many years that some white people see the current challenges to it as a serious threat to their power and control. Power and control are very hard to share, let alone give up. People will fight to the death to hold on to it. So when they're asked to give up a small amount of it, they lose their minds.

Second, seeing success and esteem as a zero-sum game—if you do better that means I do worse—shows a lack of faith on their part. Shouldn't we all be working to make that pie bigger and bigger? Then everybody does better. People who are against advancement for Blacks don't seem to believe that things are ever going to be better than they are right now. They don't trust that God's plan includes everyone, including them as well as us.

If you talk about racism with random white Americans, the first thing they're going to say is "I'm not racist." And they believe it. They get really defensive. Right now, one of the worst things you can call a white person is a racist.

A lot of them think they aren't racist because they don't use racist language, beat up Black people or pay them less, or want to see their kids' schools resegregated. They'll say, "I can't be racist! My doctor is Black! My best friend is Black!" But they don't protest racist behavior because they don't see the struggle for equality as their fight. That makes them part of the problem.

White people who don't embrace diversity are not going to get it. White people who look away from racist behaviors are not going to understand. White people who have white privilege, know it, and *feel fine about it* might get why Black people struggle against that privilege, but they don't care about that struggle because it isn't about them.

On the other hand, there are white people who have white privilege and don't know it or have it and aren't very comfortable with it. A lot of these people might be open-hearted enough to be educated about the advantages they have just because they're white. Once they understand what systemic racism is, they can step up and be true allies. They can be a voice supporting us in our struggle for true equality.

We need to create an environment where kids can feel safe about not being picked on because they're Black—or they just look different from other kids. White people are still a majority of the people in this country and control most of the public policy. That means it's their responsibility as parents and as people in positions of authority to help rebuild an America that is free from racist nonsense.

Almost nothing is being done about systemic racism. Millions of white people think that because the schools were desegregated and Black people can sit anywhere they like on the bus and there's no such thing as "colored" and "white" water fountains, the fight is over and Black and white people are treated equally. That's so far from the truth that you need a telescope to see it. Even if laws that discriminate between white and Black are taken off the books, white supremacists will find ways to shape the system so that they stay in control.

For example, it used to be that brown and Black people had a lot of trouble buying houses and renting apartments in nice neighborhoods where white people lived. The real estate people would quote them outrageous prices or tell them the house wasn't really for sale or just wouldn't show them certain listings or take them to certain neighborhoods. Apartment house managers would tell a Black person a certain apartment had already been rented and then rent that apartment to a white person.

After a while, we caught on to what the white real estate brokers and apartment managers were doing. So the banks invented the credit score, and they set it up so people of color had a harder time getting a good credit score than white people did. To this day, it's hard for a Black person to get and keep a high credit score.

So many aspects of our society are meant to keep Black people underneath white people. A Black kid and a white kid can have the same major in college and prepare themselves for the same job, but the white kid gets the job because he was able to be an unpaid intern in that field, while the Black kid had to flip burgers to earn money. When a Black student does excel at a mostly white university, white people say, "Well, she only got there because of affirmative action," and they don't take her abilities seriously. They forget about mediocre white students who were admitted because a parent or sibling went to the same school. White people have been helping each other get jobs for years and years while Black people don't have those networks. We're tired of being told we're not qualified. A lot of us are qualified, and the rest of us just want the opportunity to get qualified.

It is so sad what racism has done to America. We've all of us, Black and white, been surrounded by this thick psychological cloud, this evil, ugly mind control that's lasted for years and years, getting bigger and bigger. It keeps us from seeing each other. But we Black people, at least, are starting to fight our way out of that cloud. We're determined to get out of that fog and polluted air. It's like waking up from a bad dream. We're awake now, and we know something has to be done.

I want this generation in the twenty-first century to have more than just hope. I want them to have real opportunities that they can grab onto and move forward because they are our future.

White people can be part of the movement that is struggling for change. It isn't that hard. You just need to open your heart and see *and interact with* every single person you meet as one human being to another. Be comfortable around people who aren't like you. Start by sampling different cultures. If you've never been to a Black church, then go to a Black church. If you've never been to a Korean festival, go to a Korean festival. Just start by being around people who don't look like you and try to open your heart and learn about them.

If you want to interact with different people, you should walk into the room and sit beside a person who is different from you: someone Black or who looks like a biker or is way overweight. Approach that person as a fellow human being, maybe even strike up a conversation. It isn't that hard if you're all in the room for the same reason.

I can't be hard on people who are trying. They will never experience what it's like to be Black in America, but they try to see things from our point of view. It isn't easy for them. They have to overcome stereotypes and racist attitudes that have been ingrained over four hundred years of American history. But they are willing to have a real conversation about how to become not only nonracist but antiracist. White people who want to communicate as human to human, equal to equal, will help us point this nation in the right direction.

I give credit to white people who are sincere about trying to learn about systemic racism and willing to be active in making a difference. I think those people are on the right track. They make mistakes, but they admit their mistakes and are open to correction. You can explain to them that something they said or did was insensitive or condescending, and they'll understand that things they mean innocently can make someone feel less than equal.

Many people have called upon the government to pay financial reparations to the descendants of slaves, the way it paid the survivors of internment camps where Japanese people were forced to live during World War II. I'm not sure money can make up for generation after generation of abuse and trauma. But it's a start. The Black community certainly suffered financially because of government policies and still does. Reparations are a way the government can say that the U.S. messed up in its policies toward Black people, and this money represents our regret.

On the other hand, what America and Americans owe the Black community can't be measured in dollars. America owes us awareness to replace the cluelessness that has marked so many dealings between white America and Black America. It owes us acknowledgment that Black people have been exploited and cheated of opportunity throughout American history. It owes us transparency: to come clean about police brutality, highways that destroyed Black neighborhoods, substandard schools, redlining—everything that made Black people second-class citizens. America owes us simple respect, the respect that human beings are supposed to show one another.

It's often said that Black Americans love their country, but it doesn't love them back. That's really what Black Americans want: for their country to love them. That doesn't require reparations. It doesn't cost a penny.

Things are getting better now because so much of the bad behavior against Black people is being exposed. Twenty years ago, you were probably a member of the press, a professional photographer, or a tourist if you were carrying around a camera. Today, you have millions of people walking around with professional-quality video cameras in their smartphones. So when a police officer does something wrong, there's a good chance somebody records it.

Twenty years ago, there was also no Facebook, no Twitter, no Instagram. Now the pictures everyone takes can be posted for tens of millions of people to see. White police beating up on Black people. White folks who don't want to share their space with people of color making false accusations. It's all over the internet. Of course, what people don't get is that racist behavior and police brutality are nothing new. That kind of behavior was always happening—it just wasn't being publicized.

A lot of people have expressed worry that since Derek Chauvin was convicted, most folks will shrug their shoulders and say, "Okay, George Floyd got justice; everybody back to business as usual." But I don't sense fear from my community. I sense confidence, a feeling that we got it right this time and we're looking forward to getting it right the next time. I see a community now that doesn't carry the burden of despair, doesn't have that doubt in their eyes. They're looking forward to a brighter future. We know the war is not over and there's always another battle, but at least we won this one.

I think Perry's death brought the Black community much closer, especially in Minneapolis. Everyone is asking what he can do to help; we've learned how to take care of each other more. Outside the Black community, people are starting to ask what they have to do to make Black residents feel comfortable and treated fairly. Remember that Sam Cooke song from the sixties "A Change Is Gonna Come"? Well, change is closer than you think. Somebody ought to write a song about that.

I truly believe that in three or four or five more years, if more and more white people become conscious of their role in systemic racism, if they're willing to learn and open their hearts, we will see a real change in America. The fact that systemic racism exists, and why it exists, has to be taught in schools. Parents, especially white parents, can sit down with their children and talk about what happened to Perry and why the reaction to his killing is important. I feel hope when I see young people getting involved with issues of racial justice. Their generation is a lot more openhearted than that of their parents and grandparents—and that generation is fierce too.

Our community always has had hope for a different, more accepting America, but I can begin to see that hope becoming reality. I see school systems teaching the truth about race in America from kindergarten right through high school. I see a day when a Black girl who wants to be a nurse sits in the front row of a CPR class and a white girl sits down right next to her, a stranger who says, "Hey. What's up?" I see police officers who have been taught from day one at the academy to interact with every person they meet as a fellow human being. They've unlearned whatever "us versus them" nonsense they were taught growing up. They've stopped weaponizing skin color and predicting behavior based on racial profiling, and when they pull over a Black driver who ran a stop sign, no one gets killed.

I see Black people coming together, helping each other in community, and I see white people wanting to join that community. I see people of all races working together, sharing ideas, helping each other. And when that happens, in a climate free of racial inequality, we'll have something beautiful. More and more people will want to live in communities like ours, and they'll form those communities where they live. Then our world becomes a better world to live in, not just for us but for future generations. And if you ask me what moment changed everything, it's not just when a white police officer killed my nephew and everyone witnessed it. It's when that police officer was actually charged with the crime...and paid the price.

CHAPTER 6

The Verdict on Derek Chauvin

The verdict on Derek Chauvin came in much sooner than I thought it would. People were telling me deliberations could take a couple of weeks because there was so much evidence and so much testimony to go through. So I was in downtown Minneapolis in a store with my niece Paris Stevens that Tuesday, just the day after the jury began deciding, when my husband called to tell me that the jury had a verdict.

I called my attorney and asked, "Is it true?" And he said it was, and yes, it's unexpected that it happened so fast. He said I should go to the Hilton hotel downtown—I was so happy that we were already downtown—within the next two hours. There would be a press conference there, and I would find out which room it was in when I got there.

My hands were shaking while I was driving; I don't know how we got there in one piece. I kept muttering, "Oh, my God, thank God," because we didn't have to wait days and days for a verdict. We pulled into the first parking lot we could, and we ran to the hotel. When we got there, the lobby was full of reporters and photographers waiting for the same information as we were.

Thankfully, our loyal community leaders had taken rooms at the hotel so we could relax and reflect during the deliberations, and we went right up there.

It was getting close to two hours since I'd talked with the attorney, and finally I got a call telling us which room to go to, a big ballroom. We ran there, and people were directing press members to go into the ballroom. We talked to someone at a table who sent us to a room where the family was meeting. Almost our whole family was there, and friends of the family too and community leaders—our whole support system. It was wonderful to see them all in one place.

So many leaders from the local Black community had spent the past eleven months watching over the memorial site where the murder took place. They led protests and lobbied the city to keep traffic out of the intersection; they even picked up trash at the memorial site. All fall and winter, they stood up to people who tried to vandalize the site. They guarded it in rain, sleet, and snow. I could not be more grateful to them. I desperately wanted to share a guilty verdict with them. I wished everyone from the 38th and Chicago neighborhood had been there.

We all sat together and talked and talked, hugged and took pictures, as if it were a family reunion. There was a beautiful spread of food, but I was too nervous to eat, and so were a lot of other people; most of the folks passed by that table without taking anything. They also had a big-screen TV on the wall showing the courtroom.

It had been hard to get through the trial. As the only local relative, I promised myself I would be strong and go to the trial every day I could get away from work. I set a goal of attending three days a week. But the witnesses kept giving testimony, one after another, bringing back those nine minutes and twenty-nine seconds again and again. It was overwhelming; I felt like I was getting hit with one ocean wave after another, drenched in the tragedy until I couldn't even stand up. After the third day of watching the trial, I told my family that I didn't think I could watch anymore. I thought I was strong enough. I didn't realize that I was still grieving.

My husband arrived, and he whispered, "This is it. They're going to announce the verdict." The judge came into the court-room and said something I couldn't hear, then called for the verdict. The bailiff instructed the defendant to rise, and when he and his attorney did, we did too, as if we'd been the ones on trial. And we waited.

The judge read the first charge, and as soon as the jury foreman said, "Guilty," there was a huge roar in the room we were in. People were yelling, "Oh, my God," and some just burst into tears. I don't think I fainted, but my knees were locked, and I started to tip back a little. Luckily, my husband caught me, or I might have hit the floor.

The rest of the reading was a blur. Vaguely, I heard the judge call out the second charge and the foreman again saying, "Guilty." My nieces were crying and hugging. The whole room was in an emotional chaos. When the third verdict was read, I focused on the screen and really heard the foreman pronounce Chauvin guilty. I just wrapped my arms around one of my nieces and started crying, then some of the community leaders came over, and we were all crying together. I went over to Perry's brother Terrence, and we hugged each other and cried. We all wound up in a big group hug holding each other and crying. Our prayers for Perry had been answered.

The family was very pleased with the judge's decision, telling Chauvin, "Your bail is revoked." That meant he was going straight to prison. Another emotional outburst—someone yelled, "Yes!"

and other people started yelling, "Yes!" Another family member came up from behind me, and there was lots more crying. Our tears were tears of joy and justice, tears that come when something you've worked so hard for finally happens, tears remembering how Perry died, and tears of relief that the officer who killed Perry had been convicted. We knew there was every possibility that he might have been acquitted. History wasn't usually on our side.

I give credit for the conviction to Darnella Frazier, the young woman who captured the entirety of Perry's murder in video on her smartphone. Chauvin never would have been brought to justice—probably never would have been charged with a crime— if Darnella hadn't shot that video. Perry would be just another dead Black man, another statistic, and everything would have been business as usual the next day. Darnella was really brave. She held that phone out in front of her for ten solid minutes and got every visual, every word that went down that night.

That video is what won the case against Chauvin. The prosecutors kept telling the jury to watch the video and believe their eyes. "Believe your eyes. Just watch the video. The video shows everything that happened. Just watch the video and believe your eyes," they said again and again. And the jury did. It took the jurors very little time to decide the excuses the defense made were weak tea. They rejected the claims that Perry was ill, had a heart condition, was too close to the tailpipe of the police cruiser, died because he had drugs in his system. They rejected the idea that what Chauvin and the three other officers did represented good policing in any way, shape, or form. Even if the twenty-dollar bill Perry used at Cup Foods was fake, the jurors refused to see passing a counterfeit bill as a capital offense. They believed what they saw on the video, and what they saw was one man murdering another while two men helped the murderer and one held back the bystanders who wanted to save a dying man. I thank God every day that Darnella was there with her phone.

Remember the white girl on our school bus, who stood up for me and the other Black kids? Sometimes it takes just one person to make a difference. If just one of those police officers had stood up to Derek Chauvin and said, "This is not right; I won't let you kill this man," my nephew probably would be alive. But even through my pain and tears, I know that Perry did not die in vain.

The video gave us the victory. Still, I have to wonder: Does that mean it will become impossible to convict a police officer for killing a Black person without a video that explicitly shows the officer behaving violently, without reason? Will any Black or brown person have to have a video in order for justice to be served? How many people are in prison who shouldn't be? How many on death row? How many people we don't even know about have been killed by police, and nobody knew because there was no video?

I spoke to the press at the hotel, but I really wanted to get over to George Floyd Square and the memorial. I needed to be among the rest of the community that started the uprising at 38th and Chicago, to see as many eyes and hear as many voices as I could. And I wanted to tell them that we did this, all of us did this. It took every advocate, every activist, every person who prayed for us, who stood and walked beside us during the protests. They stayed with us although people were still being shot, killed, beaten up. So many of us in the Black community were so, so tired. That made the victory in court all the more satisfying because we accomplished it together.

I don't remember exactly what I said at the Hilton; I just wanted to let all the people there know how much appreciation I had for the love the community gave us. I spoke from the heart, and afterward, people told me it was a very powerful speech. Even media people were telling me I should take a more public role and speak for the Black community.

But at that moment, I just wanted to get to the square. This time, my husband drove the car. There were already hundreds of people out there. It reminded me of the previous year, when the memorial was first put up, and thousands of people showed up. They were already chanting his name: George Floyd! George Floyd! George Floyd! When the people in charge announced that family members had arrived, they started cheering; they were so happy to see us. It was such a good feeling. Later, a few community members told me it had been cloudy at the square all day, and when the verdict was announced, right at that moment, the sun broke through.

I walked over to the Say Your Name Cemetery, the area where community leaders had put up "tombstones" for all the men, women, and children they could think of who had been killed by police. Folks who were standing in the cemetery said it felt like the Black victims woke up from their graves, and their spirits just came right up as the verdicts were announced. When they told me that, I immediately felt this chill, and I knew it was a validation of what had happened, that Perry's spirit had risen high in the sky— as if he were saying, "Y'all did it. Y'all did it, and I can rest now."

The stage at the square was high enough that when I spoke there, I could look out over the whole crowd. I had a feeling that in spirit, Perry was in the crowd, watching me and the other people who spoke about him. I could feel the warmth and love radiating from the people in the square. "I don't know all of your names," I began and then added:

> *I realize I don't have to know all of your names. But the love that you have shown my family, that is all I need to know. That's all I need to know.*

You see, for four hundred years, we are the only race that has to negotiate for equality. Think about it. I'm going to say it one more time. We have to negotiate equality. Negotiate to rise above. Negotiate to vote. We even had to negotiate to be educated.

People in the crowd were hollering, "Yes!" and "Say it!" as if we were at a revival meeting.

You know this stuff isn't new. We have been negotiating, and when that verdict came back, it gave us validation. Validation that what we were trying to negotiate for was real.

Systemic racism is real. It is real; it has been integrated through all these systems. The judicial system, the employment system, the housing system, the education system, this is what we have been dealing with. But when we complained about it, nobody would hear us the right way. But now, but now people don't only hear us. We have validation. Today was validation that what we have been complaining about is not invented. And all of this, we, the family, we couldn't do this alone.

The community, you guys did this. When that uprising happened, you guys were there and when you came out to protect that site, to keep it sacred, you guys created a domino effect. It started here in Minnesota. The next thing I know it was national. And then the world looked here, looked at what you guys did for us, so none of this is about one person being a hero. We all did this together and made this day possible.

And I want to say, I thank you from the bottom of my heart. And like I said, I don't know all of your names, but I see you, I hear you, I appreciate you, and I won't forget you. So thank you so much and say his name!

When I called out, "Say his name!"—something I never had done before—they hollered back, "George Floyd!" I felt rejuvenated—and I felt Perry's spirit around us every time we called out.

"Say his name!"
"George Floyd!"
"Say his name!
"George Floyd!"

I went over to the garden that had fifteen or twenty names posted, tombstones for Black people who were killed by police, people like Breonna Taylor and Sandra Bland and a little seven-year-old girl, Aiyana Jones. Of course Perry's name was there too. For eleven months, I had gone to the memorial and put down flowers, lit candles, stood in silence. I went there often, but I never felt whole. I would question whether I was doing enough or doing the right things to keep Perry's memory alive. But the day the verdict on Derek Chauvin came in, I stood at the memorial and felt peace. My doubts went away. I stood there and thought, "We got justice today." Not just for Perry—we got justice on behalf of all the people killed by police who couldn't get justice. So many families couldn't get justice. I felt as if Perry were standing next to me, saying, "It's okay; you did good, Auntie." I still wish Perry was here for real, but I know he thinks we did a good job and shouldn't have any regrets over not being able to help him on May 25.

George Floyd Square turned into a real festival that evening. Somebody opened a pop-up gallery of paintings and drawings. People played music. Everybody was alive and energized—I have never felt so much positive energy. We were having a lot of fun. The press was everywhere, taking pictures, doing interviews. We didn't go home till after midnight, and then we sat up almost all night because everybody in the family was calling, and we had a million messages on Facebook and Messenger and voicemail.

Even President Biden called that day. Ben Crump, the lawyer, took that call. I give the president a lot of credit for supporting us during the trial. He's been very open about supporting policy changes to fight systemic racism, including in policing. I usually don't speak well of a U.S. president unless I've seen some proof that he's accomplished something, and all the presidents up till now haven't really done anything about racism. But Mr. Biden picked a Black vice president, and his cabinet is multicultural, has a lot of women and people of different races. That tells me he is willing to open the door to diversity in government.

It blows my mind that a white police officer is sitting in prison. That just doesn't happen in Minnesota, not to a white police officer. When Derek Chauvin was pronounced guilty, he got this shocked look on his face, as if he couldn't believe what he was hearing. I saw fear on his face for the first time. All through the trial, he showed no remorse or any other kind of emotion. But when the verdict was announced, Chauvin reacted. You could see the fear in his eyes; they got really big. I don't think he was prepared for a guilty verdict. Maybe his attorneys had told him there was a weak possibility that he'd be convicted, but up until the verdict was read, he seemed very confident. Then everything changed for him. He could not believe that he was being held accountable, and all that swagger and confidence disappeared. You could see it in his eyes.

At one point during the trial, I locked eyes accidentally with Derek Chauvin. I had to look away because you weren't supposed to have any contact with the principals in the case, but our eyes did meet. When they met, something came over me, almost like a voice saying, "Let it go." I did let it go. From that moment, I saw Chauvin not as a monster but as a fellow human being who had made a very bad decision.

I can't speak for all my family members. Some of them say they should throw away the key, let him rot in jail, but I always saw him as a human being. When Perry said, "I can't breathe," he was asking for help from a fellow human being. He wasn't going to ask a monster to help him. By telling Chauvin he couldn't breathe, Perry was seeing the officer as a human being who might help him. Unfortunately, Chauvin didn't feel the same way about Perry. He didn't see a human being when he looked at him. He mocked Perry's distress. To Chauvin, Perry was just another Black drug addict who needed to be subdued. The prosecutor brought out Chauvin's refusal to treat Perry as a fellow human. He did a great job of presenting Perry as a human being, referring to him as human again and again in his closing statement.

The trial wasn't about subduing Derek Chauvin. It was about holding somebody accountable for Perry's death. I hope it will lead to getting justice for other victims of police violence and changing laws so that police officers will understand they can't treat Black suspects like wild animals. We are human beings who deserve the same treatment as white people. We are not runaway slaves, and the police should not act as if they were slave catchers. We are human beings who deserve better, and that's what we have always wanted in this country.

Make no mistake: what happened to Perry is not just Derek Chauvin's fault. The real blame goes to the system, this broken system that has been allowed for years. It's a system in which qualified immunity has been used to paper over every mistake a police officer makes, a system that developed a police officer who had eighteen complaints of excessive force on his record *before* he killed my nephew, a system that made Chauvin think he could literally get away with murder. This broken system created officers who were allowed to repeat the same bad actions over and over and over again. Only one officer had his knee on Perry's neck, but the Minneapolis Police Department and the entire system of policing in this country killed him.

The defense lost the case because seventeen-year-old Darnella Frazier used the zoom function on her smartphone's camera and captured the entire scene, clearly showing not only Perry's death but the "Who cares?" attitude Derek Chauvin had as he killed Perry. Even knowing that recording existed, the defendant, the defense lawyers, and the police department didn't bank on losing the case because they had been getting away with crimes like that for years. But this time they've had to answer to the courts and will continue to do so. This time, the system is being laid open for everyone to see.

My heart goes out to the families who lost people they loved to police "policies" and never got justice when the killers were considered to be justified in shooting. Or were excused for "making a mistake" or "just doing their job." I pray that those families will keep their hope alive.

No matter how hard the battle is, we have to go forward because our ancestors did that for us when they took those beatings and those whippings, saw their loved ones lynched, got knocked down by police clubs and water cannons. They kept going forward in the hope that the next generation would have it better. We all have to keep fighting, because our ancestors fought for us. So many of us have stories about ancestors like my great-grandfather, who was born a slave in 1856 and worked hard to accumulate five hundred acres of land only to have it taken from him. Our ancestors lost a lot in this country, and it's our job as Black Americans to make up for their losses.

Something changed when Perry was killed. It really hit humanity. It's as if for the first time, white people opened their eyes and saw the way the police behave, the way they escalate situations so fast, the injustice we face every day. I really do think it's going to be different from now on. More and more cases are being reopened for investigation. There's more awareness of how police behave, and there's going to be more transparency. Police departments are finally getting it, and as mad as I still am, I feel that change is coming.

CHAPTER 7

One Year Out

We marked the first anniversary of Perry's death with a beautiful outdoor concert. We did Perry proud. Two or three days before the event, I was nervous because it was going to be outside at George Floyd Square, and you can never tell what the weather will be. We didn't know if we were going to be able to raise enough money to have it, and we really wanted to do something special, not just to honor Perry's memory but to celebrate his life and the Black community. We were just getting to be together after the worst of the Covid-19 pandemic, and we wanted there to be music and lots to eat so everyone could rejoice.

During the first year after Perry's death, we established the George Floyd Global Memorial on his birthday, October 14, 2020, a nonprofit dedicated to maintaining the memories of Perry and all the other people of color killed by police violence. Perry's cousin Paris Stevens and I are co-chairmen of the memorial, and Jeanelle Austin is our executive field director. We hope to raise enough money one day to build a permanent structure as a memorial site in honor of his death.

Meanwhile, the community members at George Floyd Square have committed to keeping the memorial space sacred. It has not been easy for them all, but it has been rewarding to everyone. I am brought to tears and so humbled when I watch community members care for this space with grace and humility in honor of my nephew's death. I know this whole social movement is bigger than any of us. It is about getting justice for all people killed by the hands of the police.

I've watched the George Floyd Global Memorial and George Floyd Square take on lives of their own. There is the 612 M*A*S*H team, which provides free medical care for the community, that started in a tent, staffed by volunteers who work as professionals in the medical field. Along 38th Street, next to the old Speedway gas station, community members started a book drive in an old bus depot. People in the community have brought all kinds of books for kids to read. There's also a clothing drive for people in need. One lady, Eliza Wesley, acts as the unofficial gatekeeper of the community. She's assertive and reassuring at the same time, making sure visitors feel welcome and keeping an eye out to ensure everyone's safety. The gas station is a place where people can hang out and hold meetings. One group, called AGAPE, is made up of people who turned their lives around from drugs and crime. They help provide training and jobs at the square and support troubled Black teens in the neighborhood.

The George Floyd Global Memorial put together the event at the square for the first anniversary. We had a lot of help from Maya Washington, whom our board of directors brought in. She had amazing connections in the entertainment community and knew how to stage a big event. I remember asking her, "We should get at least five hundred people in the square, right?"

And Maya said, "No, there are going to be thousands, a minimum of three thousand people, maybe up to ten thousand." She knew just how to get the word out, and she did a fabulous job.

We wanted to create a space where community members could come together and have a good time, and at the same time open their hearts to folks of all kinds. We wanted to embrace unity in our culture, but we also wanted white people to come and enjoy themselves with us.

We were worried at the beginning of the event because that morning, a block away from the square, there had been a shooting. Video recorded from the square showed people running for cover as shots were fired, and a man was taken to the hospital in critical condition. And of course the news media ran with it and made it sound as if the incident had been at the square, which it wasn't. It had nothing to do with Perry's death, nothing, and it didn't even involve the police until they responded. I prayed to God and hoped He was listening. "Please, God, I pray to you," I said, "let the world see George Floyd Square at its best."

The shooting made us antsy because we worried that something would happen at the event and get out of control, that there would be a shootout with thousands of people around. If that happened, the media would have a feast, and George Floyd Square could get shut down. Everybody would say, "See, those Black neighborhoods are terrible; they can't get together without shooting each other."

I'm sick of Black communities being labeled as dangerous places where white people don't want to go. One of the reasons I've been working on these gatherings is to try to change that perception so everyone knows our community is about respect and love. I'm not saying it's going to be a perfect community— there will always be things that happen that are out of our control.

But we can present ourselves as a thriving community where Black people work together, support each other, become entrepreneurs and grow businesses, where people can train for jobs, get health services, put their kids in afterschool program, have access to many resources. Ten years from now, it could be a Black Wall Street, a prosperous Black community that can be an example for other communities. We don't have to follow this stereotype of Black people killing each other, Black neighborhoods being dangerous. It wasn't always like that. I'm sick of hearing about Black violence and feeling helpless.

Right now, we have a sick, tired system. I know I can't fix it, let alone fix the whole world. I'm only one person. But I can work on carrying out what Perry began when he died. Perry believed in helping one person at a time by adding value to his life. He didn't have a lot of money, but he would give you his last dime. He would buy you a meal even if he didn't have enough to buy food for himself.

I can help show that George Floyd Square isn't full of wild animals the way the white supremacists would have people believe. We are a community with a purpose. I've watched many community leaders emerge from the uprisings over Perry's murder, and they definitely have a purpose: to fight for Black liberation in the wake of Perry's death. Certainly, we want to do better to take care of our Black families. That's all Perry wanted throughout his struggles: to take care of his family.

In the end, we didn't have to worry because of the shooting that morning. The community came together and checked on everyone, made sure everyone was okay and everything was okay. They were there for one another, and they stayed focused on the event.

People honored Perry in the most beautiful ways. A man from Durham, North Carolina, brought a sixty-foot quilt that had sewn onto it the names of all these Black men and women who were killed by the police. There was a special ceremony for our older relatives; they were given a golden bell and a beautiful blanket decorated with a crown that had "George Floyd" stitched into it. Then, out of nowhere, my sister Laura started singing a song of praise to God. An outpouring of love surrounded us, and we got really tearful and emotional. I looked up at the sky, and it was cloudless, the prettiest blue I have ever seen. That was a beautiful, spiritual moment for all of us. "This is so good," I thought. Everything felt perfect.

People kept coming into the square by the thousands, which brought me happy tears. There was a lot of singing: Laura Stevens, Perry's aunt, sang "We Shall Overcome," and an uncle from the father's side of the family, Ike Floyd, sang a song he had written called "Justice Be Served." He sang like a professional, and the crowd loved him, not just because he sang so well but because he was one of the family and was willing to share a song that came out of his pain. Quite a few people volunteered to showcase their talents. The atmosphere was almost like a carnival, with food stalls and activities for kids and dancing in the streets.

Everyone and everything came together on this day. Again, it's important to note that there was no fighting, there were no gunshots. Just thousands of people, Black and white and brown together, with lots of different cultures being represented simultaneously. We recognized all the Black families who had family members killed by the police. In fact, a cousin of Emmett Till— Deborah Watts, who lives in Minnesota—was there.

More than a dozen members of our family came, including some who hadn't been able to handle the trauma earlier attended.

The family members that attended were Mahalia Jones, Laura Stevens, Paris Stevens, Vins Harrelson, Tuesday Drew, Carry Wright, Sheila Shipp, Whitney Shipp, Adreonna Artis, Daeyza Stevens-Rowe, Pastor Dorian Suggs, and his wife Johnnie Suggs. There was also a special guest, the rapper and actor Common, and the Sounds of Blackness Gospel Choir performed and did an amazing job. My husband, Vins, served as emcee that evening.

My relatives and I all loved Perry differently, so we all grieve for him differently. But the tragedy gave several of us a purpose in life and brought a lot of us closer to one another. It also renewed relationships in the family; in fact, I discovered family that I didn't even know I had. I see my nephews, Perry's brothers, fighting for this cause and watching them grow and become better men and stronger men—my sister would be proud of them.

Of course, some family members haven't wanted to talk much about Perry's killing. Some of them lost other family that first year after his death, to Covid and to other illnesses, and they experienced Perry as one in a series of relatives who passed. Some carry heavy burdens of their own and just couldn't load another tragedy on their backs when life was already so tough for them. I watched some of my sisters and brothers react in that way.

I think that Perry would be proud of all of us because of the strength we've shown, each in his or her own way. We haven't made it a competition, as in who can give the best speech, who comes off best in an interview, whose presence inspires the most people to work for change. The time since Perry's death has involved us coming together for a common cause, saying that we all lost someone who was important to us, but it's a process we all have to go through individually.

It was important for my family to be there, to show the crowd that we were united and that we hadn't forgotten them after a year and recognized how crucial their support was. My sister Mahalia spread out her arms and yelled out, "This is beautiful! I love it!" And the crowd loved her right back. In fact, someone hollered back to her, "We love you! We got your back!" My almost-eighty-year-old sister gave a stunning performance, hit all the high notes, and my seventy-year-old uncle danced like he was twenty.

I was the first one of the family to speak from the stage. I walked out there and saw all those people, and I thought, "My God, Perry, you really changed the world. Even after a year, it hasn't died down." That was all the validation I needed to know that we must continue forward: we must go on. Perry opened this door for us to say, "Hey, this is something: we made this change, and it isn't going anywhere."

I talked about how difficult the past year had been and how much I appreciated the crowd's love, that we couldn't have made progress without them. "This is where Black voices finally began to be heard, here in Minneapolis," I said. "This where the boots hit the ground. Those voices created a domino effect: state to state until they were heard across America, then worldwide. It all started here in Minneapolis, and we're not going backward." It was very powerful.

People from all walks of life were standing up, clapping their hands, yelling out, "George Floyd!" There were white people dancing, Black people dancing, Latino people dancing, Africans from Africa. People were dancing on the roofs of buildings. Some people were having such a good time, they would give a high-five or a hug to the stranger next to them. It was such a great feeling in my heart. My whole family watched in awe. When we walked on that stage, we saw all these people out there for change, for Perry, and for justice for all the people who were treated unfairly.

They came to have a good time and to celebrate the future of Black America.

People are still talking about how successful this event was. Some of my friends and family have told me that they play video of the day over and over because they were so moved by it. It was all people laughing together and being in community. Everything was the way Perry would have wanted because Perry was all about community, all about people coming together in love. The white people who were there for the anniversary weren't afraid of us. They were there in solidarity with us. They saw us as fellow human beings, and they hugged us, ate with us, danced with us, clapped with us, and they seemed to enjoy themselves as much as we did.

The day ended with a beautiful word from my cousin Dorian, who's a pastor. As night fell, we gave out candles and had a candle-light vigil. I couldn't have asked for a better day. Perry was up there smiling because he saw us having a good time.

For my part, Perry's death made me have a greater purpose in life, to want to become a better person. As his auntie, I didn't have a choice. It made me look at what I need to do as a person, and it made me a stronger person, someone who speaks out more against injustice. I grew a lot that first year, and I'm continuing to grow. I was an average listener before, but now I listen more, and more intently, to what people have to say. And I never realized how much love there is in the world. I couldn't see it at first, of course, but as I came out of the darkness of those first days, I realized it was there. God revealed it to me from people around the world.

When you have so much love coming at you, not just from people in the immediate community but from across the state and around the world, it does something to you. It makes you want to give back. It gives you strength and helps motivate you to give to others who are suffering, and to move forward. I used to see the world as full of bad people in the days immediately after Perry was killed, but now I know that there are a whole lot more good people out there who care about others.

Now I'm a public figure, which often feels weird because I never saw myself that way. That wasn't my purpose. In the beginning, I just saw myself as an auntie standing up for a nephew, trying to get justice for a loved one. I had to get past the feeling that I hadn't looked out for Perry enough; later I had to come to terms with the fact that some things are just out of my control.

It is hard work being out in front of the public—in fact, it is exhausting. But it's worth it. When I see all these people with hope in their eyes, knowing that a verdict went the right way for once, and there are laws being proposed to bring about real change, it's worth it. Seeing even the possibility of achieving equal protection and equal opportunity during our lifetimes makes the effort worthwhile. I'm not struggling on behalf of just one person anymore. I'm fighting for the legacy of our entire community. This is what Perry would want us to do. As an activist, I'm still Perry's auntie; this is just a bigger way of being his auntie.

Our vision is to have a museum named for Perry that can display artwork that people have created from around the world. All the drawings, paintings, and sculptures have meanings and tell a story. It is a special way for the artists and other voices to be heard. We currently have a pop-up gallery with artwork made of offerings laid on Perry's memorial after he was killed. When I go the exhibit, I am never the same when I come out. All the pictures and drawings and found objects scream a personal outcry for help. They are saying, "Help our brown and Black children—help them."

If we can build a permanent exhibit—hopefully at 38th and Chicago—then when his brothers and sisters, his children, and his descendants come to visit, they'll be proud of Perry and know that he didn't die in vain. They'll see that a community came together to honor his life and the lives of others who died because of racist violence. I want to see this memorial built because one day I won't be here, but future generations will. It isn't about me. It's all about the future.

We didn't really have time to have a quiet moment and grieve that first year. We had to put on our running shoes and try to move forward while being pulled in all directions by the media, community groups, national groups. We'd never been in such a situation before, so we didn't know what to do or what to say. So many people approached us, and we had to figure out whom to trust and whom not to trust. It was a lot to take in. And what people don't realize is that each time we tell our story, we have to relive the circumstances of Perry's death when we haven't been able to grieve properly for Perry. It can be exhausting to relive those nine minutes every day, every time you turn around.

Even at the memorial site, very rarely did I get a time where I could sit there alone and pray. People would always want to come and pray with me, and Lord knows that's fine. What's more disconcerting is that Perry's face is everywhere: he's on a button pinned on someone's shirt; a sticker on somebody's car; he's on somebody's window or door; painted on the side of a building. He's everywhere, yet he isn't here, and sometimes it hurts to see his face again and again in the course of one day. And every time you hear that the police killed yet another person of color, it's Perry's death all over again.

Sometimes, when I visit the memorial, I sit back and watch people gather to pay their respects. They come from all over the world. One of the most distinctive objects in the square is the large fist statue, a symbol of freedom, strength, and unity, and a powerful symbol of Black pride. I often see so many people in the memorial space who are devoted daily in keeping it safe and clean. I'll watch people tidying up the memorial, sweeping out any excess dirt and picking up trash, tending to the flowers, even shoveling snow. I watch all of them carefully lay each offering in its appropriate place.

Many tourists have told me their son, father, cousin, friend, or uncle could have been a George Floyd. Perry's death connects with people across the world because it is bigger than race; it is about humanity.

Perry's presence is really strong when I am at the memorial. I often sense that he watches me when I am there. If Perry can hear me or read my mind, I want him to know that his family never gave up on getting justice for him. I am so sorry I wasn't there when he was killed.

Some of the people who visit the memorial recognize me, and when they do, they reach out with so much love and kindness. They bring nothing but genuine love and support for my family. Their tears become my tears, and we often say goodbye with a big, tight hug. Every time I leave the memorial, I always feel better than when I arrived because of the love that I received. Love is the medicine I need to survive, including the love that God has shown me.

At the square, I've also met so many wonderful community members who kept the place sacred during the uprising. They've shared story after story about how they used trash cans, chairs, cars, even their own bodies to stop people from burning down buildings. They wrapped their arms around me and received me with so much love and respect. From the beginning, I knew that I had a family for life: the community at 38th Street and Chicago Avenue.

You have to learn how to navigate all this so you can tell your story and work as an activist in a healthy way without getting burned out. You have to know when to take a break, how to say no, that it's okay to be alone. I'm still learning how to do all that. But I still walk around emotionally exhausted from telling the story over and over again.

While we've been trying to work with city officials to create a permanent memorial for Perry and other victims of police violence, the city wants the intersection of 38th and Chicago to be open for traffic again, but they've met a lot of resistance from the community. The week after the first anniversary of Perry's killing, the city removed the concrete barriers that kept traffic out of the square and the community feared the dismantling of the artwork, the offerings, and the flowers that had been planted. This created an emotional uproar; a lot of people were upset and crying, especially the folks who had brought all this beauty to the square.

Someone told me a city crew was digging up the flower garden in the roundabout that surrounds the fist, and I went out there right away. When I saw what was going on, I just broke down crying. The thought of someone removing the flowers brought the image of someone digging up my nephew's grave. I was confused, unsure of what was going on. But reopening the square to traffic didn't last. Within a few hours, the local community put up new traffic barriers and planted new flowers. When I visited the square the next day, five new large fist sculptures had sprung up, a statement of Black liberation.

The fist sculpture is really something. First there was a fist made of plywood, twelve feet tall, created and put up by unknown artists. The following January, on Martin Luther King Day 2021, it was replaced by a more permanent version in steel, designed by a local artist, Jordan Powell Karis. (The wooden fist was put up again in April in Brooklyn Center, after Daunte Wright was killed by police.) The steel fist is surrounded by flowering plants and by signs and artwork honoring Black people who experienced violence and mistreatment by authorities, people like Breonna Taylor, a victim of mistaken identity, shot by police in Louisville, Kentucky; Hardel Sherrell, who was denied care in a northern Minnesota jail and died at age twenty-seven, days after he was arrested; U.S. Representative John Lewis, a civil rights leader who was beaten in Selma back in 1965 and passed away in 2020. There are tributes to dozens of people and a lot of amazing paintings.

Almost immediately after Perry's death, three people painted a big mural of him on an outside wall, and another artist, Peyton Russell, created a twelve-by-twelve-foot black-and-white painting of Perry that faced the square. The abandoned gas station across the street from the store became a gathering place, the "People's Lounge," where folks could hold meetings or just sit and talk. In the winter, a wood fire in a steel drum would keep people warm. Someone established a small library at the gas station and a food pantry. Often on the weekends, there's a food drive to collect food for the homeless and hungry.

Everywhere there are plants in and out of pots, and mementos such as T-shirts and flags and more artwork that people have left in tribute. There's a pop-up art gallery and open-air restaurants, and about a block from the square is a grassy area that has become the Say Your Name Cemetery, with white cardboard tombstones bearing names of people who died at the hands of police. Visitors come from around the world to see it. It's full of life and very welcoming to everyone.

The businesses around the square have been very patient and have done their best to work with us. I'm sure some of the business owners are looking forward to when things will get back to normal, but there is no way we can go back to being "normal." What the neighborhood has experienced since Perry was killed has changed everyone. The new energy of the movement for racial equality has changed everyone. Sure, there are people who wish the Black Lives Matter folks would quiet down or go away. I would say to those people, "I appreciate your patience, and I understand your frustration, and I want things to thrive again. But I don't want to return to the way things were before May 25, 2020. I want things to be even better for your businesses in the neighborhood. I don't want just normal for this community—I want it better. I want it great."

We are not at war with the city officials. We respect people of authority. We just want people to communicate with us. We want to work with the city officials. We want a thriving community. We just want someone to let us know what is going on. All types of people come to the square: doctors, nurses, lawyers, engineers, cooks, janitors, retired workers. We've had hopeful signs lately: the mayor reached out and had a conversation with us. I'm not sure where things are going, but I'm glad it is open for progress.

I want George Floyd Square to be a historical site, a place where people from all over the world can visit. They can come to pay their respects, to learn about how the horror of slavery led to the culture of violence that threads through police departments, to understand why change is necessary.

God has allowed me to use my pain to become an activist against inequality and systemic racism, to help a community that was traumatized by the killing of my nephew. I am so blessed to be part of this Minneapolis community. Together, we are seeking justice and building a legacy for Perry that will last for generations. Our bigger vision for George Floyd Global Memorial includes developing educational programs and encouraging Black businesses in the community to offer internships.

This experience has given me another family, the activist community that has helped me in this difficult time. This movement is bigger than me and my blood relatives. I know the message that Perry wanted me to have, and all I am doing is standing right by it today. I just know he is looking down and is proud of me and all his family.

God is the only one that can change evil to good. I am humble and thankful that God has allowed us to witness His love around the world that has overshadowed the darkness from this tragedy. Without the outpouring of love, I could not do this alone. My family could not either. Somewhere in Heaven, George Perry Floyd Jr. is looking down, happy about the diversity programs and police reforms that have come about after his death. My great-grandfather Hillary Thomas Stewart, Sr., who was born a slave, is proudly standing next to Perry. So is his father. So is his mother. And so is mine.

I still work as a nurse. The folks at the clinic are supportive; they understand that I have a lot on my plate, and they have a lot of patience with me. I'm happy that my unit doesn't treat me like some kind of celebrity. They still see me as Angela the nurse, the tall nurse who is going to get on their case sometimes. (Everybody knows if Angela gets on your case, it's coming from a good place.) A man from another unit, Jacque, did come up to me and say he was proud of me. He asked me if I'd taken speech classes because I was such a good speaker. "I just love listening to you," he said. "I could listen to you all day, and I'm proud of you."

That touched my heart and brought tears to my eyes because sometimes when I speak, I don't know what people are thinking. I just speak from my heart and tell my story. I don't have to have everybody agree with me. I'm just here to tell the story. I'm just a tiny fraction of this effort to help make this world a better place, and I'm part of it only because someone in my family was killed senselessly. I'm only one of many people who lost someone to police violence and got involved because of that. I'm not all that special.

It would be so good to build a museum in Perry's honor. We already have so much beautiful artwork that we can put in there, paintings and murals, drawings from the children, sculpture, signs—we can bring this struggle alive for everyone who walks through the door. Every work of art, every object gives voice to someone who needed to speak out. I want people who visit to feel the spirit and energy that we've kept up since the day after Perry died, and I want them to feel different when they walk out than they did when they walked in.

If we can make the memorial site a place no one can forget, then the rest is going to fall into place. The plants will blossom every year as symbols of life and hope and renewal. We can work on building programs, but the memorial will represent our vision. When people see that museum, they'll know that we have this vision and that people in power share it. And I do believe when this happens, God is going to open the floodgates. The floodgates of heaven will open, and the future for Black America will continue to brighten.

CHAPTER 8

How My Faith Pulled Me through the Pain

When I was growing up, we only had a few toys and games to play with. We had hide-and-seek and hopscotch and other games that didn't cost anything. When you're poor, you often don't get to choose your friends because most people don't want to be around poor people. At least, that's how I felt when I was a little girl. So your friends have to choose you—and most kids didn't choose us.

As I mentioned before, I grew up in a raggedy old shack in Goldsboro, North Carolina. By the time I was in high school, the house was in grave condition, its wooden sides barely nailed together. The roof leaked, and you had to step over large holes in the porch where boards were missing. I could look down and see possums under the house, and there were two wild dogs we named Ann-Ann and Mahey-hey that we considered our pets. Our shack had three rooms and no running water; we would pump water from a well outside, and our bathroom was an outhouse. Many white people would pass by our house, and the kids and even grownups would yell, "You stink! Look at those niggers.

Their house is about to fall down!" The house probably would have been condemned if someone had reported it to the county authorities, but to us it was our home, our sweet home.

Being treated differently than the white kids, getting picked on because you're Black and poor, is extremely stressful to a child. It raises up bad feelings about yourself, and when you are young, you often don't know what to do with those feelings. Some kids are strong enough to tell their parents about it, though many kids don't, and today there are programs where children can talk to adults about what they experience. My parents couldn't give us a lot of nice things, but they gave us a lot of love and encouragement. I could talk to my mother about some of the things that happened at school. Still, I felt frustrated at times because I didn't know how to release the emotional pain, the shame of being poor and the anger over how people treated us because we were poor. So I took out my tension, frustration, and pain on an old rubber tire.

I didn't beat it or roll it—I swung on it. I loved using the big swing set at school, and I asked my father for a swing in the backyard. But we didn't have money for a swing set. Instead, my daddy made a swing from a big tire by hanging it with chains from a tree. Every day when I got home from school, I would jump on that swing, and I would pump my legs as hard as I could and swing as high as the chain allowed.

I would swing so high that it was almost an out-of-body experience. I felt free as a bird in the sky without any worries, like I could do anything. And I knew that if I felt bad, if I couldn't figure things out, I would feel better after swinging on that tire. When I got off, I'd feel as light as a feather, as if I was a bird flying high in the sky. That tire swing would be my refuge when I felt frustrated, sad, and confused.

I was a small child with a lot of dreams. On that swing, I would dream of a bigger house and a better life for my family. I would tell myself, "It's gonna be good. One day, I'll have a nice house for me and my mother. One day I'll travel to a place I've never seen." Swinging was a solitary and peaceful time for me. My mom probably worried that I'd swing so high that the chain would break, but she'd see me there, swinging and smiling and feeling free, and she never said anything, not even "Be careful now!" My father set up that tire swing out of love. I didn't question how the swing looked or how secure it was supposed to be, I just believed without any hesitation or doubt that it was safe to swing. I guess you could say the swing was part of my journey to faith because I had faith that the branch would hold the tire and chain, that I wouldn't fall off no matter how high I swung, and that I would feel better when it was time to stop.

Even before I knew much about religion, I was learning about faith. There were times I dreaded being picked on at school, but my mother encouraged me, told me to get on that bus, and that eventually something good would happen. Sure enough, the day came when that white girl stood up and told the other white kids to quit picking on me and my siblings and the neighbor kid, James. That wouldn't have happened if we hadn't kept getting on the bus. I had no choice but to believe my mother was right, that I had to keep getting on the bus because wherever it was I wanted to go in life, going to school would help me get there. I had faith in my mother, though I didn't know what to call it at the time.

I was certain that something was out there waiting for me, even if it wasn't in front of me where I could see it. That's what faith is, really: the certainty in knowing that my dreams clenched to my heart would come true. That's what has kept me going all these years. I have always had faith that tomorrow will be better.

Pain and struggle are involved, of course. Sometimes you get so tired. But even a journey filled with pain and agony and tears—a journey that tests your faith—brings so much joy when you reach your destination, because when the vision you carried in your mind and heart becomes a reality, it is such a victory. You have to keep pushing forward. My faith has been tested many times, but I have held on to it.

When I was a little older, I would walk the tobacco rows with my mother. She would tell me about the Lord. I learned to love the Lord and to pray in the tobacco rows with my mother. When we were in the fields, all we got for lunch was some peanuts, a Pepsi, and maybe a honey bun for dessert. Those things came from the white landowner; we depended on him to bring us water, soda, peanuts, and our special treat, the honey bun. That lunch break was the only break we had in a twelve-hour workday, sunup to sundown. And the hard thing was that the white farmers went back to their nice homes and had a nice hot lunch. When I look back, I wonder how on earth we survived those fields. But out there working in the tobacco rows, with almost nothing healthy to eat and no access to drinking water all the time, my mother taught me to love the Lord. Her prayers and the faith she taught me are what got me through those hot, tiresome days in the tobacco fields.

We didn't go to church much when I was a child; my mother had too many small children and needed to stay home. Also, I think, my parents were a little embarrassed that we didn't have nice Sunday clothes or money to put in the collection plate. But Mom would play gospel music on the piano every Sunday and teach us her favorite songs. So on a lot of Sundays, church was at home and its music was at home.

Mom had a large Bible with a beige cover, where she had written our family genealogy. I often saw my mom read the Bible, sometimes with a flashlight focused on the page because her vision was not the best. Mom never finished school, but she "knew the Lord," as we used to say, and she taught me about God to the best of her knowledge.

My mother loved gospel music. Her favorites were Shirley Caesar, James Cleveland, and Mahalia Jackson. She loved Mahalia Jackson so much that she named my twin sister after her. Mom never had piano lessons, but she was a gifted player. Our house was full of music every day. Folks could hear my mother's music from miles away.

Music brought Perry into our lives, because his father, Perry Senior, played all types of music at our house. He would come to that old raggedy house with some of his band members and siblings to play music with my mother as she played her piano. It sounded so good; Perry's father was a musical genius. The whole Floyd family is gifted with musical talent. Music was a powerful thing during my growing-up years. It's what brought our two families together, and of course my older sister, Larcenia Jones, married Perry Senior.

My mother told me her parents, Sophell Suggs Stewart and Hillary Thomas Stewart, were the big churchgoers in the family. My grandfather read the Bible every day; his favorite book was the Gospel of John. My grandfather drove an old Chevy, and he took us to church a few times, but mostly he went alone. He'd dress up in a suit, and he sang his heart out in the bass section of the church choir.

He was something, my grandfather. He didn't have a high school education, but he taught himself how to read music and became a scholar of herbal medicine. He knew the different leaves and herbs that helped cure illnesses and different conditions, and he would go into the woods and bring back the plants we needed if we got sick or had a cut or hurt ourselves in a fall. It was a good thing too, because we didn't have money for a doctor. I don't believe there was any health insurance at that time.

Once I was playing outside barefoot and stepped on an old rusty nail. My mother and grandfather saw me crying in pain and were afraid of me getting sick. It was uncertain whether I'd had the tetanus shot. Granddad went into the woods and came back with leaves from a cherry tree. He burned the leaves until they created a lot of gray smoke. Then he held my foot over the smoke, which he said would draw out the poison from the nail. I don't know why it worked, but the next day, my foot was fine and I could run and play as if nothing ever happened.

We would often have family reunions at a church in Coats, North Carolina, south of Raleigh. The church was the place where my great-grandfather, Hillary Thomas Stewart, started the first family reunion in the 1900s. I loved hearing about the reunions when I was young. When I attended, there would be lots of kids to play with, plenty of food, and lots of music—my family is all about music. My mother would play the piano in the church, which made me so proud.

But the important part was all of us being together. I was always amazed how much family I had. You'd see all these people, and they all wanted to get to know you. They wanted to know who you were, what generation you were from, who your parents were. Then they'd tell me what generation they were from and who their daddies were, and they'd figure out how we were related.

It was like being part of a village, a Black community of family members loving each other regardless of their flaws. The elder relatives would beam at the kids and tell us stories about the family history, which I liked hearing. As I got older and began to understand the history, I came to appreciate my great-grandfather more and more. When I speak of him, I say "Grandpa Hillary." There was so much love at those family reunions. They were a safe place for our Black family to commune, both in those early times more than a hundred years ago and when I was growing up in the sixties and seventies, and even now.

When I was a child, God was like a cross between a giant and the Wizard of Oz, if the wizard had been real. He was huge, He was king of the world, He *made* the whole world, so He could do anything. We had to be good for Him so He would save us from going to hell. He loved us. And He was white.

That's how Jesus was presented to us, as white. I was a young adult before I heard any suggestion that Jesus may have had dark skin and woolly hair. It didn't seem odd to me that God would be white. Everyone I knew, adults included, accepted that God was white. Every image I saw of God portrayed Him as a white man. Everybody in my life in a position of power was white. Everything I experienced as a child showed whiteness as being superior to Blackness, and God was the most superior being of all, so I just accepted that He was white.

Of course this originated from the attitude of white supremacy we lived with every day. We were programmed to believe God was white because white people narrated the history, not us. Black Americans were not able to narrate our own story back then. As I got older, I realized that God represents everyone, of every race, and can be any color He wants to be.

My mother had a hard, tough life. She got pregnant for the first time when she was about thirteen years old. That was the end of her childhood; she left school and worked in the fields. Being a farmworker and bearing fourteen children caused constant wear and tear on her body, and she worked through chronic back pain. She rarely bought clothes for herself. She had three dresses, and she would hand wash daily so she could save money for our clothes. She thought it was more important for us to have clothes than for her to.

Mom always made sure that we had food to eat, and she taught us how to make a sandwich out of whatever was in the kitchen. So we ate banana sandwiches, mayonnaise sandwiches, egg sandwiches. If there was nothing but bread in the house, we'd sprinkle sugar on the bread and eat that. But we never starved because we knew how to survive when we didn't have enough food. Mom would always say that God would work everything out. Her faith was really strong. At the time, I wondered how God was going to work things out, but now I understand it is more about keeping that faith and knowing that things are going to work out rather than worrying about how.

As a teenager, I didn't spend much time going to Sunday school and reading the Bible. I wasn't even baptized—that happened long after I became an adult. I was trying to find myself, to be accepted and belong, to figure things out. I wasn't sure the answers were in the church.

I didn't know what path to take, but I did know that I wanted to go to college. The question was how to finance it. My mother was determined that we would all graduate from high school, but higher education wasn't part of her vision. She couldn't help me with that. Plus my parents, as sharecroppers, were in a precarious position concerning the land they worked. When your children grow up and move away, you have fewer people working on the land, and if you can't farm the land, the owner may kick you out. I was one of the younger kids in the family, and my folks couldn't afford to hire help, so their options were becoming limited.

While I was wondering what to do with my life, I had seen all these other people going off to college, including Black kids, which made me feel kind of low. I figured they all had to be rich. I didn't understand the roles of the guidance counselor and the college counselor at my high school. I didn't have the confidence to talk to those people or apply to places, because of being advised all my life to hang back and not challenge the system. Still, I wondered, "Why isn't anybody helping me?"

One night, when I was about seventeen years old, I wrote a letter to God, asking, "Please help me be somebody." I told Him that I wanted to help get a house for my mom, but more important, I wanted to make a difference in the world and be somebody. "I know I'm Black, but there has to be a way," I wrote. Then I folded up the note, stuck it under the old tobacco barn, and hoped God would read it. Though I wasn't baptized at that time, God was very real to me. I didn't tell anyone about the letter. It was a secret between me and God.

One day, my older sister Laura came home from Iowa for a visit. I was really impressed by her, and all I could think about her was that she had made it. I wasn't going to ask anything from her, but out of nowhere, she said, "How would you like to come to Iowa?" I told her I'd love to go, and my mom gave me a look and said, "Why don't we all go?" Laura wound up taking my mom and my sister Evelyn and me to Cedar Rapids, Iowa, my first real road trip and the first time I had ever been out of the state.

I had spent my young life in a bubble of Black people and had never been to a place where almost everybody was white, so that was an extra challenge as I started my journey as a young adult in Iowa. In the course of that journey, I joined the military and learned how to endure racism in the workplace. I was able to go to college, working my way through the financial and social obstacles, going through the process of becoming someone with a formal education. I received my credential as a registered nurse and continued that career after moving to Minnesota. A few months after I moved, I received a commission as an officer in the Air Force Guard and Reserve. That was a really proud moment in my life.

A short time after my commission came through, in 1997, my mother passed away. I went home for my mother's funeral, and for the first time in years, I thought about the letter to God I'd put under the tobacco barn. After the funeral, I went looking for that old barn, and wouldn't you know, it had been torn down.

But as I was looking at the ground where the tobacco barn used to be, a feeling came over me, a voice, saying, "Angela, I did answer your prayers the day you wrote that letter to Me. You just didn't know then. Look back at your life—God answered your prayers." It wasn't long afterward that I received my commission in the Air Force, and I went home thinking, "God wants me to know that He answered my prayers." That was the moment I truly understood faith.

I'm a churchgoing woman. I'm a praying woman. I turned my life over to Christ long ago. After Perry died, I turned to prayer even more strongly because when something like that happens, prayer is all you've got. When Perry was killed, I didn't have a place to go. I didn't have privacy, that safe haven, because everybody knew what had happened. When I tried to go to work, everybody was talking about it. So that was hard, not having the privacy to deal with it. I felt so lost.

Prayer feeds your strength. The world is a cruel place, and it hasn't been fair to Black and brown people for four hundred years. When the political system and the workplace system are set against you, as I said, prayer is all you have. There was nothing we could really do about making changes in the system until now.

My faith was tested severely when Perry died, and keeping faith has been a challenge. When something like that happens to someone you love, you feel so alone, and because what happened to Perry was so public, you don't know whom to trust. Your family gives you a lot of support, but they have to deal with their own grief. Everyone is suffering and in pain.

After Perry died, I thought about his killing all the time. I would wake up in the morning thinking about it and go to bed dreaming about how he died. I kept hearing him call for his mamma and telling the officers, "I can't breathe." The images I saw and the sounds I heard on the video loomed constantly.

Finally, I remembered what my mom taught me about holding on to faith. She had always told me to depend on God—God would always work things out. That was where I would have to pull my strength from, even in a deep darkness like I was in that first year And I realized that the Lord kept showing me the images from Perry's last moments for a reason. He wanted me to keep reliving Perry's death because eventually it would enable me to get through the process of grief.

Those words "I can't breathe" sent a powerful message to the world, but it revealed another message to me. When Perry lay on the ground with that officer's boot on his neck, he was exhausted, handcuffed, in pain. He didn't have anything in reserve. But he summoned the last ounce of his strength to say, "I can't breathe"— in other words, to say, "Will you help me? Please help me."

I realize that if God could give Perry the strength to ask for help in his last moments, He could give me the strength to push forward and make something happen because of what happened to Perry. I didn't have anyone's knee on my neck. I was healthy, educated, rooted firmly in my community, with a large network of friends and family. I felt a renewed faith in God, and I used it, along with the realization of my strengths, to propel me to go out to fight for justice. My faith in God is what has fueled me through all my grief; it got me going every morning, allowed me to accomplish something every day, and helped me get stronger and stronger as time went on.

The pain was hard, of course. Often, I cried tears that I couldn't show the world. I would be at work, and the sadness would just come over me. I'd go in the bathroom and cry; I'd say, "Lord, how am I going to deal with this? How am I going to be strong enough?" It always came back to Perry and those words, "I can't breathe." How he put all the energy and the strength that he could into words while he was dying. And I knew that God gives us that strength, and I could keep going.

In those first days after Perry died, I felt his presence very close to me. I felt someone was watching me. I didn't want to tell anyone because people would have thought I was crazy. Perry was very spiritual. He may have had his faults, but he still loved the Lord. He turned his life over to God when he got clean and sober. I wasn't really surprised that I would feel Perry as a spirit walking with me, clean and sober again, back with the Lord.

When Perry's birthday, October 14, came around in 2020, I didn't know whether I had the strength to celebrate his birthday. But the local Black community surprised me with a birthday party for him. I was invited to the square, and when I walked in, they were singing "Happy Birthday" and had a cake waiting. It was wonderful to see all that love.

What I'm finding out through all of this is that not only has God shown me that I have the strength to carry on, but that He has put a lot of people in place to help me. God showed me that I'm not a one-man army, I'm not the only soldier fighting this battle. God put a small army of people in George Floyd Square making it the beautiful tribute that it is to his memory.

When we were planning the event on May 25, 2021, we didn't have much money, and we didn't have the organizational resources that other groups had that were planning tributes. We had to build from the ground up, and we didn't know how we were going to do it. But we did. We put our faith in God, and God blessed us with the right board of directors and with people who knew how to put on a celebration. And because God put everyone in place, we were able to have an incredible event, with thousands of people coming out and having a good time.

God has been with me every step of the way through this process. It hasn't been an easy one. There were obstacles, and I had to keep going through the pain of grief. Many nights I cried myself to sleep. But I'm still standing, through the court process, the trial, the interviews, the commemorations, all of it. My faith has been tested many times. But I've kept going. I am still here.

When Perry was killed, of course I asked, "God, why?" I was always taught that we don't question God because God doesn't make mistakes. When God says our time is up, it's up, and nobody's going to be late for that appointment. It's comforting to know that Perry is in heaven now, reunited with his mother and many other relatives and ancestors. But it's only human to ask, why did this happen to Perry? Why?

Through this process of building strength by trusting in God, I was able to figure out the reason for Perry's death. There was a change needed in this world. People needed to see, really see the ugliness that has been building in this country for four hundred years concerning how Black and brown people have been treated. Perry's murder, shown to the world through

Darnella Frazier's video, was the starkest portrayal of the need for change in many years.

That day, May 25, 2020, was a dark day, a painful day. But it was also a day that opened many eyes and many hearts. It gives me a little bit more peace to think that because Perry died, God allowed this world to change for the better. I don't believe God was part of this ugliness, this evil that happened to Perry, but because it did happen, God allowed something powerful and impactful to take place. He woke up the whole world to show His endless love, along with the change that needed to happen. God was able to use the evil for good.

Perry died because of his skin color and his size and the petty offense someone thought he had committed. The people who killed him didn't really see him as a person, but God did, and God made something good come out of Perry's death. The spirit of God brought people together to create a movement that would honor Perry and call, once and for all, for change in how police deal with Black and brown people. The movement spread to one city after another, one nation after another, until much of the world was recognizing publicly that unwarranted police violence against people of color must stop. Now billions of people around the world are aware of and talking about systemic racism. Even teenagers and children talk about it. Caucasians come up to me daily and want to help. They want to do something about it, and that never really happened during the 1960s, not on such a large scale. God is the only one who could move the world like that.

It astonishes me that up to May 2020, there were protests after many other Black people were killed by police, but it took Perry's murder to unite people, to ignite worldwide protest and calls for real action. Again, I credit Darnella Frazier's video for putting

Perry's violent death before the world. God had people in place to bring good out of evil. Twelve people convicted Derek Chauvin, but God convened a jury that spread worldwide.

I have a good church, River of Life Christian Church, in St. Paul, Minnesota. My church is led by my pastor, Bishop Earl R. Gilchrist and his wife, Pam Gilchrist. They both have been very supportive and understood why I couldn't attend church every week because I had so many places I had to be. But my church always has had me in its prayers. I can call it anytime and ask its members to pray for me, and they do.

It's a good-sized church, predominantly Black, but a diverse crowd of people attend. Bishop Earl has made himself available to me as needed. He is a strong pastor. He knows what it is like to go through a hard time. And he knows the struggles of what Black men have been through because of his own experiences. It's easy to discuss my nephew's death with Bishop Earl because he can relate to the man he knows as George Floyd in many ways. He assures me that God has always been with me and chose me to be the keeper of Perry's flame because He knew I was the right person to do that.

For a while after Perry's death, most folks at the church didn't know I was his aunt. We didn't have the same last name, after all. I didn't really want them to know at first because I wasn't in a good place where I could talk about it. But word got out; I think my husband told some people after two or three weeks. They were totally shocked. Once they knew, though, they were very supportive and nurturing. I needed their spiritual support because I didn't have many close family members in Minnesota except my husband, Vins. Family members would come up and visit, but they couldn't stay long. They had their own commitments in Texas and North Carolina.

Ironically, before Perry died, I was thinking about relocating. I wanted to move to Hawaii or someplace else warm, or maybe go back home to North Carolina. I felt like my time was up in Minnesota, and I just needed something different. But it was never the right time, or I'd be offered a job, but the money wasn't right; there was always a reason why I decided to stay in Minneapolis.

That's why I was still in Minnesota when Perry was killed, and I realized, "Okay, I'm here, the protest is here, the uprising is here, everything is going on here." Out of all the family members and out of all the states, I was the family member living where it all went down. Obviously, God knew what was going to happen and wanted me to be there. I'd never been really active in any kind of movement, and suddenly I was making speeches and giving interviews and being drafted as co-chair of the George Floyd Global Memorial in Minneapolis. I'd never run a nonprofit, but there I was, talking to people I didn't know, attending board meetings, making major decisions.

God already knew I could do these things, and I think it was all in God's plan for me to be in Minnesota. He allowed these things to take place because He knew I could handle them. God put all this in place because He knew that I could do it before I did.

There have been times when I've wondered, "God, why did you choose me as someone to be prominent in this struggle for equality?" I would hear a voice in my head: "Because I know you can do it." And that's why I stood strong. I've always had faith in God, and if He believes that I can do something good for His purpose, I'm going to do my best. God has guided me; He has provided me with resources, and He has put the right people in place to help me.

In the beginning, I would hear Perry's voice too. I would say, "Perry, I don't know if I can do this," and I'd hear a whisper saying,

"You can." The last time I can honestly say that I heard a message from Perry was the day of Derek Chauvin's guilty verdict. I knew I'd be expected to speak about it, and I didn't know what I was going to say. But I went to the square and spoke to the people, then I walked over to the Say Your Name Cemetery where the cardboard gravestones are, and I heard a voice say, "Auntie, auntie, you did okay. You did it." For a moment I thought my niece had said it, but I looked behind me, and no one was there. So I often wonder if that was Perry telling me I did okay.

I believe that Perry is in heaven with his mother and that when he called out for her, he could see her spiritually, though we couldn't. He's with her now, my big sister Cissy, and with his grandparents and great-grandparents. I can see them having a good time, everyone singing, my mother playing the piano. I feel like they are all in heaven together, cheering for us.

I don't think I could have handled any of this without the Lord because when we lost Perry, I didn't know what to do and where to begin. I didn't know whether I could handle so much while grieving. I was trying to be strong, trying to be an activist, trying to teach people about systemic racism. And I had to get through Chauvin's trial without breaking down. It's often said that God is going to put no more on you than what you can bear. I had no idea what that meant before Perry died, but when I look back, I realize that I'm much stronger that I used to be.

My family saw the change in me. They said that I'd grown, that I was different from the way I was in May 2020. To be honest, I think everyone in our family has grown. It gives me a sense of peace knowing that I'm helping to make a difference, and God saw something in me that I didn't know I had. I didn't know I was so strong. I didn't know anything about leading a community organization. I'm grateful that God kept me focused—eyes on the prize—and allows me to carry out His purpose.

I just want to make Perry proud of me. I'm so grateful for what I have. God gave me a community of beautiful people who love me and grew to be like family to me, and I love them right back. I got a chance to meet people from around the world, and these people stand in solidarity with me. Only God can make that happen.

I'm very humbled that God set me on this path, and I don't take it lightly. I hope that when my time is up with this role, I'll have done my best and made my family proud, and, most important, I'll have made God proud. I thank God for giving me the opportunity to lead this work in Minnesota. It's far beyond what I ever could have imagined for my life.

CHAPTER 9

The Bitter and the Sweet— Derek Chauvin's Sentencing

When I entered the courtroom to hear Derek Chauvin's sentence for murdering Perry, I was nervously hopeful. Or was I hopefully nervous? Can you be hopefully nervous? Anyway, I was both. The prosecution had asked for a sentence of thirty years; the defense, incredibly, asked for Chauvin to be put on probation and not serve jail time. To suggest probation as punishment for the way my nephew was killed was brazen and uncaring.

The assertion that the convicted officer should not do time underscored his white privilege. Chauvin had received preferential treatment since he murdered Perry. It was four days before he was arrested; he was released on bail; during the time he was in jail, he was guarded only by white officers; and when he got out on bail, the judge gave him permission to leave the state, presumably for his safety. Then his defense counsel had the nerve to ask the judge to limit his sentence to probation and time served. These moves, over thirteen months, were sickening to the Black community. Had Chauvin been Black and killed a white man, I'm sure he would have been arrested right away, denied bail, and subjected to the whims of white guards in jail, and no defense lawyer would ask for a sentence without time in prison.

It was hard for me to think well of the trial judge, Peter Cahill, because, during the pretrial hearings, my brother had put his arm around my shoulder to comfort me and to help us both be less nervous. As soon as the judge saw that, he barked out, "No movement in here." We were looking around trying to figure out who the judge was talking about, because I didn't move anywhere, and my brother didn't move anywhere. Then we noticed that everybody was looking at us (by the way, we were the only Black people in court that day), and my brother realized the judge was talking to him because he put his arm around me. Judge Cahill had jumped to the conclusion that my brother was doing something that would distract the court.

I wasn't pleased about what the judge did, and my brother remained upset about it. It was difficult for me to think of Judge Cahill as fair because he made a prejudgment about something comforting that my brother did. After that, if we were in court, I made sure that I didn't move or do anything sudden. I tried to just sit still because I didn't want any trouble. These judges have a lot of power and can have you banned from the courtroom. One elderly gentleman accidentally passed gas loudly in the courtroom, and the judge found him in contempt of court!

On June 25, 2021, after several people gave statements on both sides of the case, Judge Cahill returned to impose the sentence. He said some of the right things, acknowledging the "deep and tremendous pain" our family had suffered, noting that the pain following Perry's death flowed beyond the courtroom through the entire country. But he also said, "What the sentence is not based on is emotion or sympathy," and he also said:

I'm not basing my sentence on public opinion.... I'm not going to attempt to send any message. The job of a trial court judge is to apply the law to specific facts and deal with specific cases.

My heart sank because I interpreted his statement as meaning he would not sentence Chauvin to the full thirty years that the prosecutor had asked for. At that moment, the judge, who for all I know is a good man, reminded me of one of those white men down South who never came down hard on other white folks with the claim that it was what the law demanded.

The tone of his voice and what he said—"I'm not going to attempt to send any message"—reminded me of people I had known growing up. Many times, a judge had to decide a case in which a white person wronged a Black person and there was evidence to prove it, but there was always an excuse why the judge wouldn't impose the law to its full extent. He'd say, "I'm just following precedent in this case" (which, of course, was other white men being let off) or "I'm being lenient here because it's the right thing to do." But we all knew that the judge wasn't coming down hard on the white guy because that was a difficult thing to do in our community. He didn't want to make waves.

Even in school, if a white kid threw a rock at us, he'd be "talked to," maybe even disciplined, but not necessarily suspended, even though he'd committed a violent act and really could have hurt somebody. The teachers and the principal didn't want to make an example of the white kid, so they did just enough to satisfy the Black parents while keeping the white parents happy. Imagine if it were the other way around and a Black kid threw a rock at a white kid. That Black child would be thrown out of school faster than you can say "juvenile offender."

Do I think the white privilege inside Judge Cahill wouldn't let him go all the way with the maximum the prosecutor asked for, let alone the maximum the law allows for unintentional murder: forty years? I will let you think on that. When I heard him say that he wasn't going to try to send a message, I heard the judge's words, but I also heard the subtext in the tone of his voice. And that subtext was, "I cannot send this white man to prison for thirty years, no matter what he did."

Then the judge announced the verdict: 270 months, or 22.5 years. I'd been hoping for twenty-five, so this was below my expectations. All our family members were disappointed; it was a bitter moment for us. On the other hand, the judge could have given him even less time. In his sentencing report, Judge Cahill noted that a more usual sentence for someone like Chauvin, who had a lot of complaints about his policing but no criminal history, was 150 months, which is 12.5 years. He dismissed out of hand the request from the defense that Chauvin be given less time than the usual because he was just doing his job, writing that every Minneapolis police officer who testified at the trial, not to mention the jury, rejected that argument.

The judge added ten years to the sentence because of what are called "aggravating sentencing factors." The prosecution had listed five factors it wanted Judge Cahill to consider:

- Chauvin abused a position of trust and authority.
- Chauvin treated Perry with particular cruelty.
- Children were present during the time Chauvin mistreated Perry.
- Chauvin committed the crime as part of a group.
- Perry was particularly vulnerable to physical mistreatment.

Judge Cahill rejected the last three factors. He said the minors on the scene weren't physically threatened and didn't seem traumatized by what Perry was going through. I wish he'd considered how they might have felt later, plus the feelings of thousands of Black children who watched the video. He thought that the other three officers on the scene were actively involved, but the language of the law didn't let him label them as co-offenders. In addition, he didn't think that Perry's vulnerability to physical harm had been proven beyond a reasonable doubt at trial.

But the judge felt that the first two factors definitely applied and made it appropriate for him to sentence Chauvin to ten years more than the usual sentence. He wrote that Chauvin abused his position of authority by forcing Perry to lie on his stomach when he knew from his training that it was a dangerous position for him, by kneeling on Perry's neck, and by not offering aid when he knew that Perry was in physical distress.

And the judge certainly got the cruelty part right. He said that Chauvin's infliction of pain was uncalled for, and "it was particularly cruel to kill George Floyd slowly by inhibiting his ability to breathe," even after Perry told him he couldn't breathe. The judge also wrote that Chauvin was cruel in that he stayed indifferent to Perry's pleas to let him breathe, he wouldn't help Perry or let anyone else help him, and he kept his knee on Perry's neck even after Perry lost consciousness and even after it was clear Perry didn't have a pulse.

Twenty-two and a half years sounds like a long sentence, but when Judge Cahill announced it, I thought of all the Black men who have received sentences twice as long for lesser crimes. I thought about the brown and Black people who had inexperienced or incompetent attorneys or no legal counsel at all. I thought of all the people intimidated into plea deals carrying long sentences because they were poor or scared or mentally beaten down after hours of interrogation. I thought of people who were executed for sitting in a car while Black, jogging while Black, sleeping while Black, carrying Skittles and iced tea while Black.

And I thought of Perry, sentenced to death not by a judge, but by Derek Chauvin, labeled a criminal because he may have been holding a fake twenty-dollar bill. Last time I looked, passing a counterfeit bill, if indeed Perry did that, was not a capital offense. But Chauvin made it one, imposing the death penalty on my nephew. That's why I still feel some bitterness over Chauvin's sentence.

The impact statement of Chauvin's mother, Carolyn Pawlenty, before the sentencing was very hard to listen to. I saw the love for her son on her face as she talked about him. A mother's love for her child is very strong, and of course she didn't want her son to be in prison. She said, "I have always supported [Derek] 100 percent and always will." Every parent who has continued to love an adult child even when that child does wrong can identify with that sentiment.

But Pawlenty's statement failed to acknowledge anyone's suffering but her son's and her own. Even though Chauvin had been convicted of a murder callously carried out, Pawlenty insisted that her son was bighearted, loving, and caring—and innocent of the crime for which he'd been convicted. She lost me when she said, "I believe a lengthy sentence will not serve Derek well. When you sentence my son, you will also be sentencing me." I thought it was unfair of her to put the emotional burden of guilt on our family members, who in their impact statements had called for Chauvin to serve the thirty years the prosecutor had recommended.

She didn't mention Perry or recognize the effect that his death had on our family; even Chauvin managed to give condolences to the Floyd family. Yes, her son went to prison, but she is able to visit him and tell him how much she loves him. I can't do that with Perry, and neither can his siblings and cousins and his other relatives. Carolyn Pawlenty spoke to her living son in court that day, while no one in our family can speak to Perry until we meet up with him again in heaven.

As for Chauvin's brief statement, it came off as robotic and insincere. He offered us condolences, as if he were paying a call after a funeral. Acknowledging that we had sustained a loss is a far cry from owning up to his role in that loss and showing remorse for it. He should have been begging for our forgiveness, but he didn't seem to need or even want it. The ironic thing is, I'm working through the process of forgiving Derek Chauvin for what he did. I'm not there yet, but with God's help, I believe I can get to a place of forgiveness.

I probably shouldn't be too hard on Judge Cahill. He made the best decision that he could, given the law and the mitigating factors. He couldn't see giving a white police officer the maximum sentence, but he also wanted to do right by the Floyd family. It was a very hard thing for the judge to decide. I have faith that he weighed the evidence carefully and thought deeply about how to sentence Chauvin. It just rankles a little that he didn't want to make an example of Derek Chauvin because if it had been a Black officer ending the life of a white man, the system definitely would have made an example of him. I can't even imagine a Black man putting his knee on the neck of a white man for nine minutes and twenty-nine seconds. I'm sure a Black officer who killed a white man the way Perry was killed would have had the book thrown at him.

My family was kind of angry that Chauvin was sentenced to only 22.5 years. But as we reflected more, we realized that this is a historical moment. It is very rare that a white, male police officer is even charged with murder, let alone convicted and sent to prison. In a way, the conviction and the judge's sentence did send a message: if you're a police officer, and you kill a suspect who doesn't remotely present a threat, *and* you demonstrate indifference and cruelty, *and* it gets captured on video, you may not get away with it.

The 22.5 years isn't everything we wanted. It doesn't represent equal justice. But it's a step in the right direction. Perry's death brought together millions of Americans in protest, and Chauvin's trial, conviction, and sentence show that change is possible. Things are a lot better than they were before May 2020. I'm sad that it was Perry's death that raised people's awareness, but if it hadn't been Perry, it would have been someone else's nephew, son, brother, husband, or dad. That's why it is so important to keep going and keep fighting, because some police officer *will* commit another murder, and we'll have to make sure that he or she is brought to justice. And we'll keep fighting, with more and more people supporting us, until one day our nation really is *our nation*, with one judicial system treating all Americans equally.

I don't think that we should "defund the police." That was a premature slogan that didn't mean what it said. It refers to localities spending less money on police hardware and more on personnel who can attend to the needs of the community, people like social workers and mental health professionals. No one is talking about cutting off funding for the police. The idea is to make the police partners in protecting the lives and well-being of the people.

We need to overhaul the system of how police departments recruit, train, and supervise sworn officers, so that officers don't see all police work as "us versus them." We have to make police departments less like military installations and make military surplus like tanks and rocket launchers less available to them.

Police departments need to screen candidates for their academies thoroughly and carefully for psychological and emotional problems that will keep them from being fair and unabusive on the job. I guarantee that if somebody is abusive as an officer, abusive to people whom he doesn't even know, that behavior did not start when he entered the academy or became a police officer. The tendency toward abuse starts much earlier in life and can be traced back to an abusive or controlling parent, a neurological problem, any number of factors. The job may make an abusive person get worse, but it doesn't cause a problem that didn't exist before.

The departments also need to get rid of officers who have shown again and again that they don't respect the humanity of the people with whom they interact and turn to violence as a matter of course rather than as a last resort. Workshops on diversity and even on de-escalation of conflict aren't enough when contempt for diversity and the desire to demonstrate power are baked into police culture. Derek Chauvin had eighteen civilian complaints for misconduct filed against him before he killed Perry. He was a disaster waiting to happen.

The police unions have to get out of the way when departments need to choose between the status quo and real progress. They must tolerate the abolition of qualified immunity, the idea that police officers are immune from prosecution for crimes they commit in the line of duty. Yes, the job of police unions is to protect police officers, but too many protect officers at the expense of civilians' well-being and even safety.

Black people weren't brought into the world and raised to say, "When I grow up, I want to kill lots of people, including my own." Black people living in Black neighborhoods experience a lot of trauma: sad, jarring events that can happen from earliest childhood through old age. When you keep people oppressed for a very long time, eventually many of them will act out, often with violence. I've often heard that there are plenty of white people who really don't care if Black folks kill each other.

I hear opponents of police reform warn that people who commit crimes will take advantage of a less adversarial stance by police. They'll walk all over the police, the opponents say; gun violence will climb, and no one will be safe. They're wrong, though, because a goal of police reform is to head off crimes *before* they're committed, to take steps to de-escalate situations *before* the guns come out. No one is suggesting that police officers should be less watchful, less active in stopping crime, less present on our streets. We just want police to view the people they meet during their tours as fellow human beings—and to think before they shoot.

After the sentencing, I left the court grounds with my sister Mahalia—we had to elbow our way through all the media people—and we went to George Floyd Square. I ran into some of the community members, and we talked about our mixed feelings over the sentence. One lady was crying, saying he should have gotten the death penalty, which couldn't have happened because Minnesota doesn't have the death penalty. Everybody had all these different emotions.

I was glad I went to the square because I was able to show support and receive it as well. Every time I go there, I always feel a spiritual connection when I visit Perry's memorial. Whenever I feel down, confused, or even joyful, I go to the square as often as I can, even though it reminds me of what happened on May 25, 2020.

I think how desperately Perry fought to live on that hot cement, handcuffed, belly down on the ground, begging for help. I still have the image of his facial expressions, the huge, deep creases of agony, blood running down his nose while police officers mocked him. Lord knows how many times I've asked myself, "Why couldn't I have been there? Couldn't I have done something?" I know I would have tried. I would have been screaming at the top of my lungs, yelling at Derek Chauvin to get his knee off Perry's neck! "He's my family, my nephew, my sister Cissy's son!" I watched Perry use every ounce of energy in his exhausted body to fight for help. Perry was a soldier; he was so brave for us.

I had a long talk with Eliza Wesley, our gatekeeper. She said I shouldn't get upset about Chauvin being sentenced to only twenty-two years because all of this is according to God's plan. Derek Chauvin is not getting away with anything, she said, and you will see, there is more to come.

"Just remember," Eliza said, "this is history. Nobody thought Chauvin was even going to get charged, but we fought for that, and he was. No one thought there would be a conviction, but we fought for that, and he was convicted." Oh my God, people were ready to burn down Minnesota thinking there was not going to be a guilty verdict.

I took Eliza's words to heart. Yes, Chauvin could have been sentenced to thirty years, and twenty-five years would have been nice, but 22.5 years is something that I could live with. I could accept it and go on. When I went out to Perry's memorial site, I said, "Perry, he got twenty-two and a half years. I was hoping for more, but we didn't get it, and I hope you are okay with the twenty-two and a half years." And I felt in spirit that he was pleased because we had done so much that we didn't think we were able to do.

There are people who call us vindictive, saying that a long sentence ruins Derek Chauvin's life and it doesn't bring Perry back. But we're not being vindictive at all. Chauvin took a life, cruelly and deliberately. The punishment has to fit the crime. This has never been about hate, and it has never been about mocking anyone. It has never been about being vindictive. It is about getting justice for someone who was murdered in front of a crowd of people, begging for his life as he was slowly suffocating. There are Black men right now who are serving life sentences for murders done on impulse and with less cruelty. Vindictiveness has nothing to do with how we feel about his sentence.

Chauvin may not serve his full sentence. He could qualify for parole after fifteen years. I've made my peace with that too, because for the rest of his life he will be known as a convicted murderer, and that is far more damaging to him than the time he serves. Even if he gets out in fifteen years, he has to walk around as the man who killed George Floyd. He has to live with that for the rest of his life.

God will forgive Derek Chauvin if he asks for His forgiveness. But Chauvin won't know peace until he forgives himself, and he can forgive himself only when he can hold himself accountable and own up to what he did. I hope one day he is able to do that. In a way, the sentencing was an anticlimax because it was the verdict that told me justice had been done. He wouldn't have been sentenced to the 22.5 years if the jury hadn't convicted him on all three counts.

But I think the 22.5-year sentence is going to have an impact on judges and juries across the country from now on. The judge said he wasn't trying to send a message, but he sent a powerful message. Twenty-two and a half years is a long, long time for a police officer to serve in prison. Judge Cahill set a standard for the punishment an officer can face if he or she is proven to use excessive force that causes someone's death. Police officers who don't think twice about beating a suspect to death are getting a warning that there's a price to be paid for using excessive force. They're being reminded that they're police officers, not slave catchers, and they need to think about how they treat suspects if they don't want to share a cell with Derek Chauvin.

I understand that being a police officer is a difficult job. Whenever you are performing a service job, dealing with people, dealing with saving lives and protecting lives, it's going to come with challenges. I know this as a nurse, as someone whose job is to save and protect lives. I know, also, that there's been a reaction because of Chauvin's arrest and conviction; some officers are afraid to make arrests or use any kind of force because they don't want to be the next Derek Chauvin. They don't want to be accused of abusing their authority and get into trouble because of that. That isn't the outcome any of us are looking for; we want the police to head off crime and catch wrongdoers.

We want police to do their job. But we want police officers to approach their assignments with their hearts in the community and with a sense of serving the people, not fighting a war. We want them to go through each day with this mindset:

- I'm going to model the principles of justice and be fair to everyone.
- I'm going to use my brains and my God-given power of speech before I use my hardware, doing my best to de-escalate tense situations.
- I'm not going to abuse my power and hurt someone unnecessarily.
- I'm going to treat every person I come across, even a suspect in a crime, as a human being.

If you can't do that, if you can't bring anything to your job except the idea that everyone on the street is a potential enemy who has to be restrained or punished, then you need to take a break from policing or leave the force. What is so difficult about following the Golden Rule: treat others as you want to be treated? If you are scared to arrest people because you don't want to be another Derek Chauvin, why would you think you are going to be, and why are you comparing yourself to him? Do you have a problem with your temper? Do you have a problem with control? The only people who would say something like that are the people who recognize that they're capable of abusing their power.

If you are doing a good job as a police officer, the best that you can, if you know you are not using excessive force and you're treating everyone fairly, then you don't have a problem, and you should just go on being a good officer. Good policing isn't a choice between using excessive force or using no force at all, and the officers who act as if that's their only choice are the ones who possibly shouldn't be officers at all—or at least need a lot of retraining.

It takes a lot of courage to be a police officer, to put 100 percent of yourself on the line every day. It takes even more courage to be a police officer who risks body and soul in service of others and keeps his humanity while he does.

Judge Cahill fell a little short of what we had hoped from him, but I won't let that take me to a place of darkness. I refuse to stay in that darkness. I respect the judge and accept his decision. I know that I'm going to be okay and that my family is going to get there too. The judge may not have wanted to send a message, but you can't stop me from sending one.

My family and I, and all our allies, will continue this battle to dismantle systemic racism until it is defeated. No one can do this alone. We all need each other. Just as God brought me through that first awful year, God has led me through every day since. With thanks to God, I am no longer looking for justice in a dim, foggy light. What I have is a new light and a brighter vision about the future of our race. It's going to take hard work, but with all of us—Black, white, brown—working together, we will get to a place of real equality. Perry's death and Chauvin's conviction have cracked open the iron door that white supremacy sealed for four hundred years.

CHAPTER 10

What Must Happen Next

Dismantling systemic racism starts with awareness, and that process has begun. It's amazing how many more people have systemic racism on their radar today. Even the fact that there's a backlash shows that racism has gotten people's attention. Then comes action: going into schools, corporations, police departments, city councils, hospitals, everywhere, and showing how the "normal" way of doing business benefits white people at the expense of people of color. We need to get into people's faces—in a nice way—and get them to understand that sometimes the way they make decisions and even the way their basic hierarchies are structured keep Black people from advancing in ways they don't even realize. So first we educate people that systemic racism is a problem, then get them to see how their institutions are part of the problem.

Once they understand the problem, we can start helping these institutions become more inclusive. It's much more than in-house diversity training. It's reaching out into Black and brown communities and recruiting trainees, being less concerned with what degrees people have and more concerned about their strengths and talents. It's bringing into institutions experts who can explain why an expectation that works for white employees may not work for a lot of Black people. For example, institutions with dress codes that don't allow braids or dreadlocks or twists are telling many, many Black people, "We don't want you working/attending school here, no matter how talented you are." Even if a Black person doesn't wear her hair like that, how welcome is she going to feel if the subtext of the dress code is "Look as white as possible"?

Racism didn't end with school desegregation and the passage of civil rights legislation in the 1960s. A new form of segregation developed when white families fled from cities and public-school systems to private schools and white suburbs. Inner-city public schools often get the least experienced teachers and a smaller selection of academic classes, hampering the opportunities of bright Black and brown students. The Voting Rights Act of 1965 put an end to certain practices that kept Blacks from voting, but the Supreme Court has gutted that law, and state legislatures across America are passing new laws to restrict ballot access, laws aimed directly at voters of color. Luxury housing has displaced thousands of Black renters from their neighborhoods.

No wonder so many Black people feel like caged animals. Keep them penned up long enough, they'll start to go at each other in competition for the few crumbs the power structure throws to them. This is on top of being told their story is not America's story and the way they present themselves is inferior to the way white people present themselves. It exists alongside an American narrative that prizes "rugged individualism" over cooperation and material wealth over human relationships. These factors undermine the values of family, cohesion, and mutual support that have kept Black people going in this country. You can't pull yourself up by your bootstraps if you don't have boots. What hope do we have?

We won't break out of our cages until we have the same access to quality education, job training, transportation, voting, and a dozen other institutions that white Americans have and take for granted. That requires effective programming, and programming costs money. We have resources within our own community, but we need white people to be allies: to teach us how to write grants, how to make the most out of our schools, how to achieve political and economic clout. That's how the white establishment can help us best.

This can happen. Since Perry's death, I've met any number of white people who are comfortable with Black people, at ease walking the streets of our communities and entering our churches. We Black people have had to navigate the white world all our lives, and now we see white people willing to navigate ours. The more comfortable we become with each other, the more we can get done.

It isn't enough that white America has had this wake-up call concerning systemic racism and the need to reform policing. We have to focus on how people need to take action, what they need to *do*—both white and Black people—so that we don't slide back, so that we make progress and make the world better for everybody.

We need to end the denial about racism and call out racist behavior when we see it. White people know when they've seen or heard something racist but they've looked the other way. They'll say, "I don't think that's quite right," but they don't do anything about it. I don't know why treating people fairly is so difficult. If we all treated each other with respect, regardless of skin color, it would solve a lot of the world's problems.

First, we have to take a long look in the mirror. We have to be honest with ourselves and about how we treat other people. That starts with being honest about how we were raised and how our perceptions were filtered through those of the people who raised us. We need to look back at our upbringing, not to use it as an excuse for racist thinking or a reason to say, "I was raised right, so I can't be racist," but to understand what we have to overcome or to build on.

My mom had something that made her different from other kids: she had a deformity, six toes on one of her feet. Other children picked on her because of that. But, she said, there was a girl in her class named Ethel Mae Baldwin who stood up for my mother when she was bullied for having six toes. In return, my mom took up for Ethel Mae when kids picked on *her*. My mom and Ethel Mae became best friends for life, staying close into their seventies, when my mother died.

I heard the story about how my mother and Ethel Mae became friends many times while I was growing up, so many that it was ingrained in me. I don't know if my mom even realized how much that story sank into me, but it taught me to stand up to anything that was not right, even if standing up for the right thing represented a risk. My mom also insisted that people be treated fairly and equally. I grew up with a twin sister, and sometimes people would try to give her things that they didn't give me, or vice versa. My mom would always stop them, saying, "If you don't have something for both girls, don't give it to just one." From early childhood, she was instilling in me how important it was to treat people fairly.

She didn't use words like "equality" and "discrimination." That wasn't her approach to simple fairness, to use fancy words. She just knew it was wrong to treat people badly because of who they are or make fun of someone who's different than you. She planted that seed in our hearts about fairness. That's how I know a lot of the ways people behave really start from what they were taught at home, seeing the world through the stories and beliefs of your elders, even if you don't understand all of it at the time.

And if you can't get those values from home, you must be willing to listen to people who are different from you—and listen with an open heart. That's where you start: if you're not willing to listen to other people's perspectives, nothing will change for you. When we allow our minds to be open, then we can hear their words, and the door opens for understanding. It takes your own vulnerability to embrace other people's differences, but that develops when you start to listen.

Difficult as it is, white Americans must admit that white privilege exists. They have to acknowledge that being white means other white people will not judge you for the color of your skin. If you present as white, other white people may judge your grammar or how you dress or what you do for a living, but they won't make assumptions about you on the basis of your being white. You may not feel as if you have power, and compared to other white people, maybe you don't, but you have privileges—some subtle, some not even visible—that people of color do not.

Often, when someone uses the phrase "white privilege," the white person hears, "You had everything handed to you. You didn't work for what you have." Then that person gets defensive and responds, "I grew up poor. I put myself through school. Nobody gave me anything. I worked hard for everything I've accomplished." But, again, that isn't what the phrase means, and it isn't what people of color think—at least I don't. White people also think eradicating white privilege means they'll have to give up something, sacrifice something that we Black people will then take from them. That isn't true either. The only thing we're asking white people to put aside is the idea that because their skin is lighter than ours, they're superior to us.

I understand how difficult it is when that feeling of superiority is challenged. Here's an example. When I was working on my degree in psychology, there was a white girl I hung around with. We were in the same class, and we studied together. In one course, I happened to get a better grade than she did. We'd both done well: she had gotten an A-minus, but I got an A-plus, and that really bothered her. She actually said to me, "I was supposed to get a better grade than you."

I said, "What are you talking about?" and she said, "Well, you got an A-plus and I got an A-minus, and I have to admit, it made me feel bad that you got a better grade than I did." I realized that she responded that way because she was white. I'd heard it all before. She wouldn't come out and say it, but I knew what she meant. I felt betrayed because I worked so hard for that grade.

Most of the time, Black people have to work twice as hard as white people just to be recognized as competent. To hear my classmate say that she was supposed to get higher grade than I did made me realize how unequal we were, that she saw herself as superior to me, entitled to a higher grade because she was white and I was Black.

Another thing that makes white people want to hold on to their privilege is the feeling that if they give it up, we Black folks are going to treat them the same way they've treated us. First of all, that's ridiculous. We want equality, not revenge. Second, most of us weren't raised to treat people that way. Third, what are white people giving up? They didn't deserve that privilege in the first place.

They didn't deserve to be given a warning after being pulled over for a broken taillight when a Black driver got a beating for the same thing. They didn't deserve to go to high schools with robotics labs and twenty-five Advanced Placement courses when

Black youngsters were in classrooms without enough desks and often substandard materials. It's all an accident of birth: where you were born and to whom you were born. White Americans are lucky, not deserving, when they get better treatment than Black people with the same brains and the same skills.

Because white people have controlled the narrative of history, they believe and even teach that it's their right to control our nation's wealth and its governments. When Barack Obama was elected president in 2008, Black people were so excited, hooting and hollering, that we forgot to ask, "What took so long?" White men had been presidents for 220 years when Obama was inaugurated. That's the way most Americans assumed it would be till the end of time. No wonder a huge number of Americans got upset when a man with darker skin was elected president. They thought only white men deserved to be president.

And no wonder white people have been nervous at the prospect of Black students getting educations comparable to those of white students. Educated people and smart people aren't fooled as easily as the slow and ignorant. They see the manipulation and exploitation and crookedness for what they are, and they're less willing to be messed with just because white people think they deserve to hold all the power. I remember my mother telling me that one of the white high school teachers in our town said he would quit before he taught a Black student (but he used the n-word). When all the schools were finally integrated, some of the teachers did quit.

There are people who say that white privilege is a lot for white people to give up. It is not. I've been dealing with the results of white privilege all my life, and so have most other Black Americans. I know the prospect of Black people having the same rights and status as white people makes many white people uncomfortable, but the truth of the matter is that you've been comfortable for too long.

We need you to educate yourselves, and not just by reading, though there are many books on how you can recognize racial inequality and become an antiracist yourself. We need you to open your heart and your social circles to people of color *as equals to you*. Look around your network: clubs, PTA, neighbors, your child's sports teams, the sports you play. If you've ever so much as had a pleasant conversation with someone of color at a soccer game or a school open house, while walking your dog or in line at the market, take the next step and ask that person out for coffee or to your next barbecue. You don't have to become tight friends, but this is what happens:

- Your kids see that you socialize with all types of people and learn that behavior as normal.
- Your neighbors see that you socialize with all types of people and—just maybe—might start thinking about the sameness of the people they know.
- You learn about different cultures and subcultures, enriching your life with their beauty and variety.
- You get to chip away at stereotypes people of color may carry about *you*.

Some people will say that it's a lot to ask Black people to accept a social invitation from white people, especially because Black folks are so tired of explaining Black attitudes to white people. They'll say it's like we're supposed to act as if 450 years of slavery and Jim Crow never happened because you invited us to your barbecue. I take a more pragmatic view. Every step toward inclusion is important, including the barbecue—as long as we get the same brisket your white neighbors get.

If there is a time for change to happen, for America to move in a direction toward racial equality, it is now, the 2020s. It's long overdue—it never should have been necessary—but it has arrived. The murder of my nephew Perry put an awareness of systemic racism in people's minds and hearts. Millions of people have shed their blinders and are looking at the reality of racial profiling with clear, open eyes. Civic leaders are instituting diversity classes for public employees because they want police, firefighters, social workers, clerks to stop judging people by the color of their skin. People are engaging in conversations about race and racism who never gave it a thought five years ago. Members of the generation that is just starting to move up in influence are impatient with racism and willing to change the system, and the Black members of that generation are fierce and won't take "no" for an answer. This is the time for us to move forward.

I like the way things look right now because so many white people are pouring out their hearts to me, asking what they can do to help. They're standing alongside us in numbers we didn't see sixty years ago, protesting and calling for fundamental change.

Some of the truths I put forth are hard, tough truths. But I don't hate white people, and most of the other Black people I talk with don't hate white people. We weren't taught to hate. And the change we seek may not even happen in full during my lifetime. I want to leave a world that's on the road to being a place where race simply isn't a consideration for opportunity and advancement: no white privilege, no Black privilege. I want to have a world where I don't have to hold a sign that says Black Lives Matter. I truly believe that we're heading toward that world. That hope is beautiful to me, and my vision of a society where equality and respect for all people are taken for granted is a beautiful thing to me.

I'm often asked if the Black community can ever forgive white America for how whites have treated Blacks. We're already doing that. We've been forgiving white people for more than four hundred years. Not everyone is able to forgive, but most Black people are religious, and most religious Blacks are Christian. Forgiveness is a basic tenet of Christianity. Whenever we've been hurt or oppressed, we've always found a way to forgive and go on. We couldn't have accomplished what we've accomplished and developed our culture as much as we have if we stood still and hated.

Dylann Roof went to a historic Black church in Charleston, South Carolina, in 2015 and shot up a bunch of people studying the Bible, killing nine of them. The story of the murders lasted way past the usual few days because of two things: Roof's lack of repentance and the willingness to forgive Roof shown by some of the survivors and relatives of people killed that day. Not all the families forgave him, but several did. "We have no room for hating, so we have to forgive," said the sister of one victim. This is a lesson of the Black church: to remain human in the face of inhumanity directed at us.

When you have been treated as property, and after that trauma as a second-class citizen, I think it actually becomes much easier to forgive. We know how it is to be treated as less than equal; we almost expect it. Some of us have loved ones who were killed by white police officers. I have ancestors who were lynched. There are Black people who saw their loved ones shot and killed in front of them, just as their enslaved ancestors saw loved ones killed before their eyes. Black Americans had to accept those things and learn to modify our lives on a daily basis to live with them.

We knew, though, that we could not let our trauma curdle into hate. We have been frustrated and angry—and have displayed that anger and frustration, which is only human. But we always knew that we cannot carry that hate. It is bad enough that we have to carry the attitude that we're not as good as white people. It is bad enough that we have to carry the wounds, large and small, of systemic racism. And now you are going to add hatred on top of that?

Our goal must be to go forward and bring about change so that our children and their children can have a better life, and we can't do that with hate. We keep the fight for equality going fueled with forgiveness and love, because what we're fighting for is about love and acceptance. It doesn't make sense to fight hatred with hatred. I think white people have trouble understanding this. They have a harder time understanding forgiveness than Black people do because they are members of the privileged race. They haven't had to deal with systemic racism, so they have a lot less to forgive.

My mom would get frustrated about being poor, and she knew that white people looked down on us and sometimes confronted us with prejudice and disrespect. But she didn't carry hate in her heart. She just wanted us to keep going, and she would encourage us constantly, saying, "You can do it," and "You can be anything you want to be. I don't know *how* you are going to do it, but keep the faith and don't give up." That isn't a hateful message. Hatred would have just stood in the way. Mom wanted her children to live in a world where no one cares what color you are. After all, God created a diversified world, with all different types of celestial objects, plants, trees, animals, human beings. That's the world Mom read about in her Bible and wanted to pass on to me, a world that loves what's different about us as well as what we have in common.

People worry that the activism spurred by Perry's killing will fade away, and his death will become just another story. I don't think that will happen. My nephew's death made an incredible, huge impact on the world; I think, in the long chain of incidents where white police killed Black folks, his death was the turning point. People sent condolences and statements of support from around the world, from places I never heard of. There was an outpouring of pain and grief, along with a sense of "This is where it has to stop."

When I go to the memorial, I see people crying on each other's shoulders. They seek comfort and healing, not just for themselves but for their country. The day Perry died changed the world because for the first time, enough people could not look away and could no longer accept the ways things are. It opened and changed people's hearts. Dr. King was murdered too, and Nelson Mandela spent decades in prison, but their societies changed because of their sacrifices.

Since Perry's death, I've noticed white people being a little more conscious of Black people's presence, less likely to not see them. These days, if a white person bumps into me, she'll say, "Oh, I'm sorry, I didn't mean to do that," instead of acting like I wasn't even there. Or someone will hold the door and let me go through first instead of just assuming I'm going to hold the door for him. I've experienced a lot of "After you"—"No, after you" this past year or so.

I feel like there are more white people paying attention now, going out of their way to correct the wrongdoing toward Black America and being more transparent about white privilege. Of course there's a big difference between being polite and being antiracist, but I have noticed many white people going out of their way to show that we're on their radar.

You can argue that saying "Excuse me" or "After you" doesn't mean a white person wants a Black in-law or is more likely to hire a Black person for an office job. On the other hand, you have to start somewhere, and if these white people are just pretending to care about Black people's feelings, well, you can fake something for only so long. I truly believe there are white people now who have gotten the message from what happened to Perry, and they really are trying to show an increase in consciousness. The people who are putting up a façade will be exposed sooner than later.

Earlier, I wrote about a shopkeeper who didn't want to let me come into her store late at night. A similar incident happened during the pandemic. My husband and I went to the grocery store, and we found that it was closing early because of Covid. We got there about 7:55 p.m., and the manager said, "Sorry, we're closing in five minutes." We said, "Okay, we understand," and we turned around to leave. Just then, a couple of white people walked by us and headed into the store. My husband said to them, "They're closing in five minutes. They're not going to let you in."

The white guy said, "Yeah, yeah, yeah, yeah, yeah," as if our experience didn't apply to him. And they marched right past us into the store. My husband said, "Wait, I bet he gets in." Sure enough, they were admitted to the store.

The next morning, I called the store manager. I said, "Sir, I'm one of your Black customers. I watched white people welcomed into your store just before closing after my husband and I were sent away. I'm not trying to be a troublemaker, but you need to educate the person who was in charge, because when we saw white people going into your store after we were asked to leave, we felt like he was discriminating against us because we were Black."

I wasn't trying to come across as an angry Black woman, and I wasn't trying to sound like a militant. I just wanted him to know how I felt. I'd like to think I'd have made the same call if I'd been white and had seen Black people turned away. The manager was very polite. He said, "Thank you for telling me. I will talk to the night manager about it."

That's the way to handle things. Everybody needs to step up and talk about what they see, because otherwise all these behaviors continue, and nothing changes. The protests are great. It's wonderful that people are going into the streets and seeking their rights. But on a day-to-day basis, wherever racism happens, whether it's at work or in the street or in a store or a hospital or anywhere, if we see it, we have to say something. That's the responsibility that everyone has.

Sometimes—and I realize this is difficult to do—a white person can fight racism by acting against his or her personal interests. Let's say you apply for a job just for the heck of it; you have the basic skills necessary, but the work will be a stretch for you, with a steep learning curve. Your real hope is that the company will have a lower-level opening. A Black person applies for the same job, and her résumé shows experience that will let her step right into the job and do it well on the first day. You get the job because the HR director and the immediate supervisor think you're a better "fit" for the company. (It's well known that people responsible for hiring are better disposed toward people with whom they're comfortable, and that usually means someone of their own group. That "implicit bias," as it's called, may not even be consciously felt.)

It's hard to turn down a position that pays better and represents a big jump in your career, but that's the antiracist thing to do to counter the racism (conscious or not) of the hirers. You weren't expecting to get that job, and the ethical thing to do is ask, "Was mine really the best résumé?" Let them know that you appreciate the offer, but if someone truly qualified was in the running, that's the person they should hire.

The same goes for assignments within the workplace. If you're white, and you get the plum assignments, the most interesting ones or the tasks that lead to advancement, while your Black colleague gets the most tedious or insignificant assignments, that isn't right. It's your job to say, "Hey, these assignments you're giving me are great, but Tim deserves some of these jobs to do; he's just as good at the work as I am." The truth, if you focus on being fair and treating people equally, you will always win, regardless of your race, your religion, and your sex.

No one today is accusing white people of condoning slavery. In fact, that's the point: racism is more subtle today than it was in 1865 or 1921 or 1964. It happens in a thousand quiet ways, through voter-suppression laws, through neighborhood gentrification that prices out residents of color, through underfunded, overlooked inner-city schools. Much of the time, it doesn't even happen in a public setting for all the world to see. But these laws and practices, added to assumptions about race, combine to create a system where racism can survive.

The main thing is to speak up when you see injustice. You can't remain silent and expect anything to change. The marches and demonstrations are great, but where's the follow-through? People have to do more than carry signs and banners. Yes, white people are opening the doors, but will they be receptive to the changes that may come because of the doors they opened? And will they stand up to the millions of Americans who still don't want this change to come?

If Perry could join this conversation, if it had been someone else killed outside the convenience store on that night in May, he'd be talking about community, people coming together to help each other. I think he would say that we all need to get it together and work together as one. Help people when they are down, no matter what race they are. If they need food, feed them. If they need clothes, give them some clothes. And put God first. Perry wasn't a civil rights activist prior to his death. He was just a Black man who had challenges with his sobriety. But if Perry were still with us, if another man had died the way he did on May 25th, he would be right out there doing the big and small things to fight racism.

We all must stand up and do what is right, like the white girl on the bus back when I was thirteen. I don't know where that girl is today, but the memory of that day and what she did stayed with me all these years. She used her voice to make right what she knew was wrong. People like her are reasons I haven't been walking around angry for the past fifty years. I could have walked through life hating, but she stood up and used her voice.

If she hadn't spoken up to the other white kids, I might have been miserable on the school bus until I graduated from high school. If the three officers with Derek Chauvin had pulled Chauvin off my nephew, Perry probably would be alive today. It's all about standing up and doing the right thing.

CHAPTER 11

How Can We Teach Our Children to Be Antiracist?

It isn't clear that the problem and the results of systemic racism will be solved in my lifetime. But I do think there's a clear and wide path for everyone who nurtures and works with children—parents, teachers, babysitters, day care operators, coaches, camp counselors, clergy, and many more—to develop a new generation of young people who are proactively antiracist. Social science says we can do it. Antiracist schools and communities *show* we can do it. It won't be easy because it involves millions of American adults breaking old habits and establishing new ones. However, we can do it.

I'm not directing this chapter toward people who can't separate a person's worth from the color of his skin. I doubt anything I say to a true racist will change her mind about judging people by color. I'm writing to the people who haven't been aware of the effects of systemic racism until now. I'm addressing the folks who really don't know when they're committing a microaggression (but want to know so they can stop) and the ones who boil inside when someone makes a racist remark—but don't say anything.

Many people wouldn't openly use a racial slur or discourage their children from bringing home Black friends. But they're comfortable with a passive role, and ending systemic racism involves a critical mass of Americans becoming "antiracist," willing to call out racial injustice wherever it occurs. Without real activism and effort, without pressuring legislators and governors to pass laws against discrimination and corporate executives to revamp their hiring practices, lasting change cannot occur. We have to be willing to leave our comfort zones, even to the point of taking to the streets.

The first misconception that needs to be thrown out is the idea of "colorblindness." Whenever a white person says to me, "I don't see color; I look at the person inside," I know that person isn't telling the truth, whether he knows it or not. I remember years ago when a white co-worker took her first trip to Africa. I asked her, "How was your trip?" and she began telling me about her experience holding an African baby. When she held the Black baby in her arms, she said the precious little one would start to cry immediately. It was like her skin color was a shock to the baby. When she gave the baby back to the Black mother, the baby would stop. The mother was seen differently in the baby's eyes. Over a few days, the baby became accustomed to the way the white woman looked and eventually did not cry when she held him again.

I don't think anyone is born a racist, but babies as young as *three months old* can differentiate between people who look like their primary caregivers and those who don't, and that includes their skin color. Toddlers, beginning at thirty months, can tell when someone is showing a racial bias—and can develop it themselves. Just think: If a white child already perceives you as different, imagine what happens when a racist parent starts to teach that white child negative stereotypes, such as "All Blacks are lazy and violent people." This stereotyping leads to fear and hatred, and if parents also use slurs like the n-word, it only adds fertilizer to growing inequality.

When children recognize their differences amongst one another in school or at home, it opens the door for parents and teachers to plant the seeds of love and fairness. That's why we all need to push back against the idea that being white is the ideal.

That pushback begins with being willing to talk with kids about race, which sends many people out of their comfort zone right from the get-go. You can't treat race as a taboo subject just because the prospect makes you nervous. Pushing it aside, saying, "We don't talk about that," makes discussion of race sound like something shameful. If you aren't sure what you want to say, write down some notes about your own feelings and what you want to express to your kids. Make sure what you plan to say matches how old they are. Then practice what you want to say before you say it, whether it's in front of a mirror or with a trusted friend.

With young children, you want them to talk about race—but not everywhere and where it's appropriate. Many Black people have had the experience of seeing a small white child point at them and hearing him yell, "Look how dark that lady's face is, Mommy!" When I lived in Iowa in 1983, I had a little white girl say a similar message to me. I had just left a store, and a young white lady was walking with her child of about four or five years old to her car. The child could not stop staring at me. She stared at me and pointed her finger and said, "Mommy, why is she so dark?" The white lady told her, "Be quiet and get in the car."

That could have been a teachable moment for that little girl if her mother had introduced her to me. This would have allowed her to see that it was okay. Even if I was darker, I was a human being just like her. When we as parents ignore our roles in creating a fair and safe place for kids, it ends with an awkward way to open a conversation about race, doesn't it?

If you want to do your part in creating a nonracist child, but you aren't ready to talk with Black people on the street, you can ward off embarrassment by training your kids to show "respectful curiosity." That's where you encourage them to ask questions about people who don't look like them but to ask them quietly, to you. (The same applies, by the way, to kids who are curious about any physical characteristic, such as height, weight, clothing, or hair.) If you can answer those questions in the market or at the playground, great; or it may have to wait until you're in the car or at home. But if a child opens a conversation about race by showing curiosity, be prepared to answer her questions.

Picture books can be a great way to celebrate Blackness with children young enough to be read to. It's tempting for a white adult to choose a book that celebrates diversity by showing children of many different skin tones. But books that show Black children being secure in their environments and their Blackness or acting bravely to achieve a goal (such as freedom from slavery) can be even more powerful. Children who aren't Black who look at such books can recognize how the Black character's experience and culture are different from theirs and how they are similar.

These picture books, which begin with board books for toddlers, are also useful for Black adults who want the children in their lives to feel good about themselves in a world where they're the minority. Poet Ruth Forman wrote her first board book, *Curls*, after her daughter came home from preschool and said that she wished her hair was straighter and her skin was lighter. Forman was shocked, but the hurtful experience opened a new path for her; after *Curls*, she wrote another board book, *Glow*, about Black boys. "It's important for white children to see Black and Brown children happy and smiling," Forman said after *Glow* was published. "But it's important also for Black and Brown children to be proud of themselves."

With both younger and older children, the hope for racial equality can be presented as an issue of fairness, which is important to kids. Babies as young as a year old can perceive a situation as fair or unfair. By the time children are preschool age, they have a well-developed notion that whatever one person has, the next person should have it in equal measure. That can apply to:

- *Respect:* "Why does the teacher talk nicer to the white kids than to the Black kids?"

- *Treatment by authorities:* "Why did Devone get suspended and I didn't? We both pushed the guy."

- *Opportunity:* "Why aren't there any Black kids in the top math group?" Children are not fans of injustice once they know about it.

You can also call on a child's empathy to fight against stereotypes. Have your children figure out that the idea that all Black (or Asian or Latino or white) people act in a certain way can't be true. Explain that when you predict people's behavior based on their skin color or appearance, you're making them less than human. What if the person being stereotyped was your brother or sister? What if it were you? How would you feel, and what would you do?

Once kids are old enough to be aware of tensions in the community, you may have to respond to news about things like police shootings and street demonstrations. Try not to turn away children's anxiety or curiosity; ask them directly what feelings they have about what they've heard on the playground or seen on the news. Address their fears and correct misconceptions. If a child asks why violence against Black people keeps happening or why Black people still face inequality after all these years, try using a visual model to represent the difficulty of the problem. Have the kid wind string around your hands and fingers so it's difficult even for her to undo the string and free your hands. Mummify the child in toilet paper and tell him to get out of it. He'll see that it's a lot harder to get free of a problem than it is to create it.

Painful as it may be, you also need to look at your own tendencies and actions. Do you live in a neighborhood where almost everybody is white? Do you socialize with people of color? Do they come to your house as guests? Maybe you're someone who likes to choose the path of least resistance, not make waves, not take on society's burdens. You're entitled to choose that way of life, but it isn't a mindset that will serve your children well. You may be an authority figure in a child's life, but you need to display empathy as well and see situations from the child's point of view.

Even if you're afraid to anger neighbors or colleagues by taking a firm stand, you'll be a better role model for your kids if you do. Acknowledge the mistakes about race that you've made in the past. Don't shrug off racial tensions as "the way it's always been and the way it always will be." There has been progress in how America has treated its Black residents over four hundred years, and there is plenty of opportunity for more. Look outside your own neighborhood and become an advocate for many different types of people.

Most of all, gather whatever strength you need to call out people who are comfortable, even supportive, of racial inequality, and prepare yourself to become a visible, unambiguous supporter of racial justice. That doesn't mean telling off your boss even if she might fire you, and it doesn't mean you have to wear a Black Lives Matter T-shirt to work. But it can mean asking your head of HR whether there is any way for the company to discourage people from using racial pejoratives. It can mean showing up for a peaceful march or rally—and helping it remain peaceful. You can still support your local police force, but part of that support can be calling for funds to be spent not on tanks and rocket launchers but on reform-oriented training and the deployment of mental health personnel as first responders. It means letters to the editor and to your legislators, attendance at meetings or classes, possibly organizing like-minded people where you worship.

The hardest thing about becoming an antiracist, especially if you shrink from confrontation, is facing people in your social sphere and educating them regarding racial justice. You need to be ready to object to any racial pejorative or joke on the spot, telling people (even people you love, like your kids, siblings, or parents) that mocking Black people with labels and quips is unacceptable, and why. You'll be accused of not having a sense of humor, but you can reply, "I have a great sense of humor. I just prefer jokes that are meant to be funny to *everyone.*"

Be ready, also, to face down "what-aboutism." That might come up when you state, say, that police often react to peaceful protests with violence, and the person you're talking with says, "Well, what about all those antifa people in Portland who destroyed businesses?" After you acknowledge that violence on the part of any group is wrong, have your facts lined up, such as "Left-wing extremists are a tiny fraction of protesters against racial injustice" and "Even the most extreme anarchists, if they commit a crime, commit it against property, not other human beings."

You actually may make some headway in bringing people a little closer to your point of view if you learn the basics of conflict resolution (what used to be called "fair fighting"). These include staying calm, being willing to listen, sticking to one topic, and acknowledging the other person's feelings and opinions and showing respect for them. Steer clear of language implying that you think the other person is stupid, ignorant, or evil. The idea is to appeal to your opponent's best self, not to shout down opinions you believe are wrong-headed.

Becoming actively antiracist isn't easy. It requires study, which takes up time you may not have, and a little courage, a muscle you may not have used much lately. But it's worth doing. And you can do it.

The role that schools should play in developing antiracist children has become a topic of especially heated debate during the past couple of years. It began with the publication of "The 1619 Project" in the *New York Times*. In August 2019, the newspaper published a series of historical essays about how the enslavement of Black people in the United States has had an influence on many aspects of American life—government, business, medicine, the criminal justice system, culture—since the first permanent European colonists brought enslaved Black people to today's Virginia in 1619.

The *Times* produced a study guide for teachers to use in classrooms with "The 1619 Project," and the prospect of schools teaching about the far-reaching effects of slavery on American institutions made many people uncomfortable. Opponents argued that school is not a place where children should learn in-depth about wrongs white people imposed on Black and brown people. Schools should be neutral about race, they said, teaching that all races are equal now and people of all races are of equal value. It shouldn't focus on any one racial group—and it shouldn't take up very much of the social studies curriculum.

The problem with this neutral "colorblind" approach is that it trains children basically not to think about race as important, not to dig into racial attitudes in America's past, and not to talk about race. Silence about race reinforces the status quo; it does nothing to refute the idea that whites are first among equals and there's nothing wrong with white people being in charge. A lot of schools have mission statements that celebrate diversity and support racial justice, but the schools themselves, in what they teach, tend at best to create nonracists, not antiracists. Schools need to be much more proactive in teaching students, especially white students, about race, racial identity, and what true racial justice looks like.

Many federal, state, and local governments, including school boards, and thousands of parents have become frightened of what in-depth knowledge of slavery's repercussions might unleash. That fear has brought a fierce attack on critical race theory, the study of how the workings of major national institutions affect the lives of people of different races. Leaders and parents who are afraid of critical race theory claim that teaching about the history and causes of American racism not only will make children hate America, but it will cause children to feel sad and will cause white children to hate themselves just because they're white.

In other words, critical race theory is being boiled down to a buzz-phrase meaning "White people are bad." It isn't that at all. It isn't even new: critical race theory has been a concept discussed in American universities for years. Wikipedia posts this detailed definition:

> *Critical race theory...examines social, cultural, and legal issues primarily as they relate to race and racism in the United States. While critical race theorists do not all share the same beliefs, the basic tenets of CRT include that <u>racism and disparate racial outcomes are the result of complex, changing and often subtle social and institutional</u>*

dynamics rather than explicit and intentional prejudices on the part of individuals. [*accents mine*]

Notice that critical race theory doesn't blame individual people's prejudices for how American society and institutions have treated people of different races in different ways. Applying critical race theory to public school classrooms simply means not glossing over the truth of how the white majority related to minority groups throughout American history.

For example, children should learn that many of the founders and early leaders of the United States were owners of slaves as well as talk about the accomplishments of Blacks and whites. That's just the truth.

Similarly, teachers can celebrate the landmark civil rights legislation of the 1960s while noting that in recent years, state legislatures and courts have been trying to reverse much of that lawmaking. They can discuss the origins and spread of Jim Crow laws taking rights away from Black people without blaming the white sharecroppers who didn't live much better than Black ones. I'm sure there were many good white farmers in those old times, after slavery was abolished, but how often was it documented that they spoke up for Black America? Many whites feared being ostracized by their own race or being labeled an n-lover, which they felt was not a good option for them. Whatever the reason, it never helped anyone in the end. These are all discussions that should be had. Children will always ask why things happened the way they did, so we must show and explain to them a better way. They can describe anti-Black riots and lynchings and the effect they had on Black people without holding all white Americans responsible for the actions of others, and discussions about how some whites tried to free slaves and how many more chose to be silent.

Critical race theory isn't some insidious kind of mind control, and it doesn't threaten the authority of parents. It promotes the idea that the more people know about the effects of racism, the less likely those effects are to continue or to happen again. Isn't that what most Americans want?

So what should schools communicate about race?

They can start by affirming that there is nothing inappropriate in talking about race; everyone identifies with at least one race, and race is an essential part of who a person is. They can teach that although a tiny part of your DNA determines your skin color, race is not really a matter of biology; it can't make you "naturally" one way or another. Race is what's called a social construct, an *idea* (not a reality) that has been created and accepted by the people in a society. In other words, when white people say that Black people are lazy or lacking in brainpower, it's because enough people in their society agree that Black people are that way. That doesn't make it true, and it's the school's job to point that out.

By encouraging discussion of race and presenting race in a positive light, schools can provide a safe place for kids to be who they are. They can persuade students to be aware of their attitudes and to look beyond their own experiences. Adults in schools can help kids manage racial stress and learn how to stand up to racially motivated bullies. Teachers can help their students analyze what they see on the news and especially on social media, which can contain enormous amounts of racial bias and misinformation.

This shouldn't be difficult to achieve, although many state legislatures and school boards are trying to tamp down discussions of race and the truthful "warts and all" presentation of American history. Just as antiracist individuals are obligated to call out racism, schools have to develop the will to face up to white parents and politicians who want children's bubbles left intact and prefer history to be taught with a glossy coat of whitewash. Even if parents are setting good examples at home, kids spend a huge amount of time in school over the years. What children of all races learn and experience in school is crucial to how they will respond to racism as adults.

We still have a long, long way to go in the fight for Black people to have truly equal status with white people. But I have to say, for the first time in my lifetime, I have hope that this will happen for children of color who have already been born.

The events of May 25, 2020, robbed me and my siblings of a nephew and deprived other members of my family of a brother, a father, a cousin. We'll never be the same. Perry's death was a needless tragedy that happened because one man failed to recognize Perry as a human being and other people didn't value Perry's humanity enough to save him. At the same time, though, Perry's murder touched off the biggest demand for civil rights that we've seen since the 1960s.

Perry's story is similar to that of so many people in the Black community. Many of the elements of his childhood—absent father, moving around a lot, extreme poverty—are all too familiar to Black people. So was his chosen road out of poverty, through athletics, and so was the fact that that road didn't pan out. He had to leave college, where he'd been recruited to play football, and go to work to help support his family.

This is why Perry's life, not just his death, resonated so deeply for Black people. We could all relate to every step of his journey: the instability, the lack of a father figure, the conflict between getting an education and taking care of one's family, not to mention sometimes making the wrong choices. To be treated like a monster instead of a person accused of a petty crime—we've had that happen to too many of us. Perry's life was all too typical of the problems and pressures Black people face. We could all see ourselves not just in how he died but also in how his life played out.

White outrage over gratuitous police violence against Blacks was a long time coming. Eric Garner, Michael Brown, Trayvon Martin, Tamir Rice, Ahmaud Arbery, and too many others to name died at the hands of police officers or self-appointed vigilantes primarily because they were Black. Each death was followed with outrage, protests, and street demonstrations by Black people and non-Black allies. But Perry's death took everything to another level.

We can make progress only if we all look on each other as human beings. When I walked into the courthouse the first day of Derek Chauvin's trial, I was really nervous. Security was tight, with blockades set up and police watching everything everybody did. I entered the courtroom, and right away I saw Mr. Chauvin at the defense table. He was wearing a business suit and a mask because of the pandemic, but I recognized him by his eyes. Our eyes met for a few seconds before I turned away. Yes, I saw him as the white man who killed my nephew. But I also saw a human being standing in front of me.

I think that's the key: that people really are beginning to understand that folks who aren't like them, who don't live lives like theirs, are still human beings deserving of life and dignity. As a younger woman, I might have said that things would always stay about the same. I can't say that anymore. I see a lot of things changing. I've seen people standing up for their rights and I've seen people gather every day at George Floyd Square in Minneapolis, people holding down that space for justice. It has become a sacred place, with white, Black, Asian, Native, all different kinds of people saying, "Enough hate. Time to move forward."

One way or the other, Perry's death was the tipping point. Because of the inhumane way my nephew died, it created a whirlwind that changed people across the globe. Millions were moved and touched by what happened. Black people who grew up keeping quiet realized that they couldn't be quiet anymore. White people who thought racism wasn't their problem decided to make it their problem. Hundreds of thousands of people began marching and protesting, not just in our nation but in different countries all over the world. Even some corporations have taken a stand against racism because they understand that racial abuse is bad for business.

Things have begun to change. Chokeholds and other uses of excessive force by police are being banned in one locality after another. Thousands of people are lobbying for the elimination of immunity from criminal prosecution for police and the establishment of alternative personnel for traffic stops. Body cameras are being turned on earlier and left on longer.

This change does come at a crawl, though, and is opposed by powerful police unions and legislators. Why did it take Breonna Taylor's death to make people realize that police shouldn't just barge into people's homes like it's wartime? Police had been doing that for years. How did the officer who shot twelve-year-old Tamir Rice see him, with his pellet gun, as a deadly threat? What was the Rochester, New York, officer thinking when he pepper-sprayed an emotionally distraught nine-year-old girl when she was already handcuffed and in his patrol car? And why, six years after Eric Garner gasped, "I can't breathe," in New York City, did one more person—my nephew—have to gasp out those same words in Minneapolis? (Let alone the victims we never heard about.) These attacks on Black people by police continue as slowly, slowly departments begin the process of reform.

There hasn't been enough change since I was a child in North Carolina. I saw family members who shouldn't have gone to prison go to prison because they had no money for bail or a lawyer. That hasn't changed much. I've seen the robotic, inhumane mentality of the police up close several times. We all have, especially if you are Black and live in America. When my patients have gone to court to face criminal charges, I've seen the judges who won't go against the police. And today I see state legislatures passing laws that make it harder for Black people to vote, enabled by the U.S. Supreme Court when it gutted the Voting Rights Act in 2013.

One of the most difficult things I came to terms with is that there are no more options for Perry and me. There are no longer any options to call him. I no longer have the option to see him. My options to make plans with Perry are no longer available, and when that finally sunk into my heart and mind, it left me with a huge void to deal with in all this chaos and the aftermath. I am left with questions that only I can answer. Where do I go from here? How do I deal with the press? Who do I trust? Who will help me? Can I do it alone?

I wish I could talk to Perry; I could not answer any of these questions at that time. I could only trust in God.

When things finally settled, one of the first things I did was go visit the memorial alone. I had been there with my family, but I just wanted to go alone because I knew that my family would not always be there. I had to find a way to be strong for me. Sometimes when I visit the memorial, I sit back and watch so many people gather from around the world to pay their respects. I often say, "Perry and I should be at Thanksgiving dinner with the family. Instead I am coming to his memorial in Minneapolis."

One of the things that catches my attention is the large fist statue at George Floyd Square. It's a symbol of freedom, strength, and unity, and pronounces a powerful solidarity of Black pride. I often see so many people in the memorial space who are devoted to keeping that memorial safe. I watched several people tidying up the memorial and sweeping around any excess dirt and picking up things that did not belong.

I watch all of them carefully lay each offering in this original place. Many tourists have told me their son, father, cousin, or uncle could have been a George Floyd. Perry's death connected with so many people across the world because it was bigger than race—it was about humanity. Perry's presence is felt so strongly when I'm at the memorial. I often sense he watches over me when I am there. If Perry can hear me or read my mind, I want him to know his family never gave up on getting justice for him. I am so sorry I could not have been there to help when he was being killed.

Over a year later, we finally got justice. I have some peace knowing the police officer was found guilty and was sent to prison for it. "Perry, I hope you can rest in peace now." Thousands of people from all over the world visit the memorial every month. Some know who I am, some don't, and when they do, they have reached out with so much love and kindness. It's nothing but genuine love they have for me and my family. Their tears become my tears, and we often leave with a big, tight hug. I call it a "Holy Ghost" hug.

Every time I leave the memorial, I always feel better than when I arrived, because of the love that I have received—it's the medicine that I needed to survive. It is God's love which He has shown.

At the square, I met so many wonderful community members who kept the place sacred during the uprising. They shared story after story about how they used their bodies, trashcans, cars, or whatever they could to keep the space sacred by stopping rioters from burning it down. The George Floyd Square community wrapped their arms around me and made me feel so much love and respect. That day, I knew I had a family for life. The community at 38th and Chicago.

Today, I am the co-chairman, along with George Floyd's first cousin Paris Stevens, and board member, executive director Jeanelle Austin, of the George Floyd Memorial. The community members at George Floyd Square are extremely committed in keeping George Floyd Square sacred. It has not been easy for them, but it has been a rewarding experience for everyone. I am brought to tears and humbled when I watch the community members care for this space with grace and humility in honor of my nephew's death.

I still have hope for the future of civil rights in the American Black community. Too many Americans, Black and white, will no longer remain silent in the face of police brutality. More and more people are recognizing that Black people's struggle for justice is their struggle too. A growing population of young people are ready to break down barriers between ethnic groups and bring about a better world for everyone.

I was a baby when Dr. Martin Luther King Junior spoke about racial justice to a quarter-million people in 1963, and like many Blacks, we fought ever day to be equal and stay alive. When Perry was murdered, I became an activist in order to help get justice for him and other Black people. We are born into this role of a self-activist, fighting against inequality because of the "injustice" of being Black. If we don't advocate for ourselves, no one else will.

Today I get calls to speak publicly, to be in the forefront of the movement that is trying to make this country and the whole world a better place for everyone. I would have been much happier not to be a public figure and have Perry back. But that's not how life has turned out. So I have to feel, and carry the message, that good that can come out of tragedy. If there were no hope, my nephew's death would be in vain. His gasps for breath, his plea for life *can't* be in vain. I won't allow it to be in vain.

The fight for racial justice and equality is huge, and it's still in its infancy.

Use your voice. I don't care if you have to scream at the top of your lungs—you're your voice! Make yourself heard and make a difference.

Lift your voice and be heard!

Lift your voice!

That's how the world will heal.

APPENDIX

Victim Impact Statement

This is my impact statement, which I did not get a chance to read to Derek Chauvin. Maybe one day he will get a chance to read it and know how I felt that day.

STATE OF MINNESOTA	DISTRICT COURT
COUNTY OF HENNEPIN	FOURTH JUDICIAL DISTRICT

Case Type: **Criminal,**
Court File Number: **27-CR-20-12646**

State of Minnesota,
        Plaintiff,

VICTIM IMPACT STATEMENT

Vs.
        BY ANGELA HARRELSON, AUNT

OF GEORGE P. FLOYD, DECEASED

Derek Michael Chauvin,
        Defendant.

My name is Angela Harrelson, and I am the aunt of George "Perry" Floyd. To the family, he was known as Perry to us. To the world, Perry was known as George Floyd. Perry's mother, Cissy, (Larcenia Floyd) was my big sister.

Perry was my nephew. I watched him grow up since the age of four or younger. His mother, Cissy, and her children often lived with us in North Carolina, off and on to get on their feet. Cissy was a single mother trying to raise three kids. Throughout the years, I watched a small boy from learning how to pump water from the well to hearing from my sister, Cissy, tell how Perry was a popular star athlete in High School. His goal was to be an NBA star, but there were tough times and Perry fell short. One thing that never fell short was his love for his family, especially his mother. Perry stood almost 6'4" tall. Under all that height was a man with humbling spirit that would give his last dime to help anybody.

When Perry moved to Minneapolis a few years ago, it helped us become closer. We were each other's only close family members in Minnesota. I was so excited about this relocation to the Twin Cities. I was like a kid in the candy store! All I could think were all the fun things we were going to do together like travel and having family dinners/reunions. Little did I know, I did not have enough time.

What happened to Perry on May 25th, 2021, was one of the darkest times of my life. I felt like I let my sister, Cissy, down because I was not there to help him. I served my country in the military to protect and serve. I save lives as a nurse, but that one day, May 25th, 2021, I slowly watched Perry die on T.V. from my home, shocked, scared, angry, like the bystanders, I felt completely helpless. When he cried out for my sister, Cissy, the word mamma, then Perry, was gone. When I think of this scenario, I often begin to cry all over again.

Several times I thought about leaving Minnesota to get away from chaos, pain, turmoil, and grief but my nephew is everywhere, on somebody's building, wall, and all over the world. All I could think about at the time, is starting over because Perry's death has left such a huge void in my life. My life will never be the same. Some people think that Officer Chauvin's conviction sets things right. All

I really wish for is to turn back the clock to the day before Perry was murdered and have him back with us. But what this conviction does mean is that police officers, like Mr. Chauvin, will be held accountable when they think they operate above the law and dictate themselves as the judge, jury, & executioner. I do not hate Mr. Chauvin. I hope that his soul will be saved one day through God's grace. All the families have suffered a loss. I want Mr. Chauvin to remember Perry's words, "I can't breathe." All Perry wanted was for Chauvin to help him. He asked Mr. Chauvin for help because he saw him as a human being. No one will ask a monster for help. I just wished Mr. Chauvin would have seen Perry as a human being. Because of that, Mr. Chauvin must be held accountable for his actions. May God be with you.

Angela Harrelson

Acknowledgments

Vins Harrelson, my husband, who has been a rock through all of this. Not in a million years would I have imagined us going through something like this together. Your support and understanding is amazing! Whatever I need to get through those difficult days, you always find a way to make it easier because I know you want me to succeed and most of all be happy. One thing I know is that none of this would be possible without you, my family, and God in this difficult journey. You have consistently provided a loving and supportive environment because of your faith in God.

Laura Stevens, my elder sister, who saw greatness in me and invited me to her home in Iowa. I was a skinny, scared country Black girl, but I knew you were there to support me on my new journey. When I first started this book, I was not sure if everything would fall in place, but you prayed for me all time. You'll never know how much I appreciated coming to George Floyd Event Anniversary 2020 in Minnesota, singing the song "We Shall Overcome." You always will tell me the right way, no matter what, because you put God first.

Mahalia Jones, my better half, fraternal twin sister, who was so wonderful in helping me with some of the childhood stories. Writing this book and sharing stories brought back so many of our memories growing up together in Goldsboro, N.C. Yes, I remembered our pet dogs, Ann Ann and Maheyhey Puppies (named after us). Through this rough year, you brought laughter and smiles whenever I needed them, and it was always on time to help me get through this book.

Parsis Stevens, a precious goddaughter, my niece, who continues to amaze me daily. You have given so much of your time, after so many long and tireless hours working as a R.N., along with building the GFGM organization in Minneapolis. Thank you for just being a ride-or-die partner and family member I can always count on. From the beginning of the movement, you stood with me, and we are still standing together.

Subrina Montgomery, when I came to Minnesota, I was searching for family and discovered a beautiful cousin—you—inside and out. I learned from you that our grandparents were brothers and sisters, along with so much more about my family roots because of your spectacular research on our family history. You are the best!

Michael Levin, when the idea of me seriously writing a book came, I had no idea where to begin and God pointed me in your direction. You had no idea who I was at first, but you took a chance on me because you believe not just in me but in my message about Perry to the world. Through the writing process, it often became cathartic—almost like therapy sessions as I wrote in one of the most difficult times in my life. I consider you a mentor in this industry and a dear friend.

Esther Leah Tennenbaum, you were truly amazing in helping me work through each chapter. I appreciate your patience and allowing me to be my authentic self. I know sometimes it was long, and I often wondered if we were ever going to get through all the pages. You would always say, "We will get it done. It will be fine." Thank You!

Acknowledgments

I want to thank my literary agent, **Steve Troha**, for never giving up on me or on this book. And I would like to thank everyone at the publisher, **Post Hill Press**, including David Bernstein, for acquiring the book; Heather King, for her excellent management; Kate Post, for her insightful copyediting; Donna DuVall for her thorough proofreading; and everyone else involved in making this book a reality.